Analytical Grammar

Level 3
Parts of Speech
Instructor Handbook

Created by R. Robin Finley

ANALYTICAL GRAMMAR.

888-854-6284
analyticalgrammar.com
customerservice@demmelearning.com

Analytical Grammar: Level 3, Parts of Speech Instructor Handbook
© 1996 R. Robin Finley
© 2022 Demme Learning, Inc.
Published and distributed by Demme Learning

analyticalgrammar.com

1-888-854-6284 or 1-717-283-1448 | demmelearning.com
Lancaster, Pennsylvania USA

ISBN 978-1-60826-658-6
Revision Code 1122

Printed in the United States of America by CJK Group
 2 3 4 5 6 7 8 9 10

For information regarding CPSIA on this printed material call: 1-888-854-6284
and provide reference # 1122-11012022

Table of Contents

Level 3 | Parts of Speech

Why We Learn Grammar

Children begin learning the grammar of their native language long before they can speak it fluently. Even a toddler knows that "Dad ate pizza" makes sense, while "Pizza ate dad" is silly! Unlike other subjects, we already know the grammar of our daily language—even if we don't know that we know it. The key, therefore, is two-fold:

- Apply labels to the different parts of speech and grammar. We know grammar; we just may not know the names of things or why they are organized in certain ways.

- Understand how to use different language and grammar in different situations. While formal situations call for more formal language, the grammar of our everyday, informal language is not incorrect. Correct grammar changes depending on the situation. Just as a person using informal slang might be judged in a formal business setting, the opposite is true: using formal language in an environment where casual language is the norm would seem strange.

These two components combine to make us better writers and, therefore, better communicators. Consistent use of grammar and proper use of punctuation helps keep written information flowing easily to the reader. With a mature understanding of grammar, students are better able to share their increasingly complex thoughts and ideas in a clear, understandable way.

Getting Started

Some grammar "rules" are unbreakable. A sentence must always have a subject and a verb, for example. However, in many cases, rather than "rules," they should be looked at as "guidelines." Even professional grammarians (We do exist!) disagree on things like what a prepositional phrase is modifying in a sentence. Sometimes we even disagree with ourselves from day to day! This is okay. A sentence can be grammatically correct even if there is disagreement about how it is parsed or diagrammed. If your student has enough grammar knowledge to make an informed argument as to why they believe a certain answer is correct, it's a win—give them credit and move on.

The goal of each lesson is that students acquire enough familiarity with the topic that they can achieve 80% on the assessment. *Analytical Grammar* is intended to be an open-book curriculum, meaning that students are encouraged to use the lesson notes to complete all exercises and assessments, so this should not be a difficult goal if students are completing the exercises. Once a level is completed, the lesson notes and Application & Enrichment pages are designed to be removed from the book to create a grammar handbook that the student can use for life.

Grammar is a cumulative process. While new parts of speech will be addressed in subsequent lessons, students will continue to practice what they have already learned, and new skills will build upon that knowledge.

Analytical Grammar is just one component of a complete language arts program, which should include literature, writing, and vocabulary or spelling. By dividing the program into five levels, students are able to spend a short time focusing on grammar, then concentrate more fully on another component armed with the skills to improve their communication. Completing a reinforcement activity every couple of weeks and using the review lesson, when available, prior to starting the next level ensures that students' skills stay sharp.

Components

Analytical Grammar is separated into five levels:

Level 1: Grammar Basics: elementary introduction to the nine parts of speech.

Level 2: Mechanics: elementary guidelines for punctuation and word usage.

Level 3: Parts of Speech: complex information about parts of speech and their interactions

Level 4: Phrases and Clauses: advanced work with more complex components

Level 5: Punctuation and Usage: in-depth information about punctuation and word usage

For each level, you will need these components:

Student Worktext

- *Student Notes* provide instruction and examples for each topic
- *Exercises A, B, and C* give students plenty of practice in applying their new knowledge
- *Application & Enrichment* activities provide weekly instruction and practice with functional writing skills
- *Assessments* are always open book and provide an accurate measure of proficiency
- *Reinforcement* worksheets are provided to keep skills sharp between levels

Instructor's Handbook

- Page-by-page Student Worktext copy with solutions for all student work
- Instructor tips with additional explanation on possible points of confusion
- Item-by-item scoring guide for all assessments

30-Week Schedule

The study of grammar is just one part of a complete language arts program. Your student is expected to progress through the *Analytical Grammar* lessons at their own pace, then continue to practice grammar skills while studying another area of Language Arts.

Lessons			Reinforcement	
Week 1	Lesson 1		Week 11	Break
Week 2	Lesson 2		Week 12	Exercise 1
Week 3	Lesson 3		Week 13	Break
Week 4	Lesson 4		Week 14	Exercise 2
Week 5	Lesson 5		Week 15	Break
Week 6	Lesson 6		Week 16	Exercise 3
Week 7	Lesson 7		Week 17	Break
Week 8	Lesson 8		Week 18	Exercise 4
Week 9	Lesson 9		Week 19	Break
Week 10	Lesson 10		Week 20	Exercise 5
			Week 21	Break
			Week 22	Exercise 6
			Week 23	Break
			Week 24	Exercise 7
			Week 25	Break
			Week 26	Exercise 8
			Week 27	Break
			Week 28	Exercise 9
			Week 29	Break
			Week 30	Exercise 10

An *Analytical Grammar* Week

Most *Analytical Grammar* lessons are set up in the same manner: a page of notes, three exercises, an Application and Enrichment activity, and an assessment. The following is a suggested schedule for completing one lesson a week.

Monday

Read over the lesson notes with your student.

Have your student **complete Exercise A**.

- Work the first one or two sentences together, then have your student complete the rest. Remind them that they can use the lesson notes as needed throughout the week. Encourage them to ask for as much help as they need.

Tuesday

Review Exercise A.

This should take no more than 20 minutes.

Discuss only those mistakes that relate to the lesson you are working on.

- For example, if you are working on Lesson 1 Nouns, Adjectives, and Articles, just look at the words that are supposed to be marked. If your student has marked a verb as a noun, you can safely ignore it. These kinds of mistakes will correct themselves as students go through the program.

Have your student **complete Exercise B**.

Wednesday

Review Exercise B.

Have your student **complete Exercise C**.

Thursday

Review Exercise C.

Read over and discuss the Application & Enrichment activity.

Have your student **complete the Application & Enrichment activity**.

- Note that Application & Enrichment activities include important concepts for grammar proficiency, so don't skip them.

Friday

Review the Application & Enrichment activity.

Have your student **complete the assessment**.

- Remind them that it is open book and they should use the lesson notes as much as necessary.

The following Monday

Correct the assessment together.

- You read out the answers as your student crosses out any incorrect answers.

- Then, using the scoring guide found in the Instructor's Handbook on the assessment key, total up the correct answers and record the score on the test.

- Achieving 80% or higher on the assessment demonstrates that the student has acquired enough familiarity with the topic to move on.

Now, **introduce the next lesson** and start the process all over again!

Potential Activities

Parsing

There are only nine parts of speech. Some parts will always have the same job in a sentence. Others can fill a variety of roles depending on how they are used. Identifying the parts of speech helps to narrow down the roles they may play. You will never find an adjective acting as an object, for example. Adjectives are always modifiers. On the other hand, nouns can do many different jobs in a sentence. Identifying parts of speech is called parsing. This is the first step to identifying the job that a word is doing in a sentence, since it helps students narrow down the possibilities.

	art	adj	adj	n	av	pp	art	n	pp	art	n

Example: The quick brown fox jumped (over the dog) (in the road).

Short Answers and Fill-in-the-Blanks

Some exercises include short answer and fill-in-the-blank questions. These include activities like providing definitions, identifying a word's job in a sentence, and revising sentences to have proper punctuation.

Diagramming and "The Process"

Diagramming a sentence can strike fear into even the most experienced grammar student. That's why we break it down into an easy-to-follow series of questions that we call "The Process." In small increments, by answering yes/no questions about the sentence, students learn to diagram increasingly complex sentences until they are confidently creating elaborate diagrams. Your student will be well prepared for the challenge. Some students enjoy the satisfaction of putting all of the parts of a sentence into their proper places.

We don't, however, diagram just for the sake of it. Diagramming visually demonstrates the structure of a sentence. It can clarify a relationship between two parts of speech like no amount of words can. While it is important to practice each new skill learned, once a student can demonstrate confidence with the part of speech, diagramming can be reduced, and you may find that your student doesn't need to complete every sentence in every exercise. It is simply a tool to support understanding of the parts that make up a sentence's structure. By Level 5, when grammar concepts are secondary to punctuation rules and guidelines, diagramming is put aside, but the knowledge acquired remains.

Application & Enrichment

On the fourth day of each lesson, students will complete an Application & Enrichment activity. These activities are based on grammar, punctuation, and writing skills. They aren't usually directly related to the topic of the lesson, but they cover important concepts that will benefit students as they develop their writing skills. These activities provide a break from the lesson content, allowing students' brains an opportunity to store the grammar information they are learning in long-term memory. While these activities are intended to be fun and informative, they introduce and practice important skills and should not be skipped.

Assessment

On the fifth day of a lesson, students have an opportunity to show you and themselves what they have learned. They will be asked to complete exercises that are similar to the daily exercises. Points are assigned to each section; they are found in the Instructor's Handbook with the solutions. The points are intended to be a measuring stick for how confident the student feels about the material. Remember, your student can use their lesson notes to complete the assessment. They should not try to complete it from memory, without support. Before moving to the next lesson, the goal is for your student to receive at least 80% on the assessment. If this goal is not achieved, we recommend that they repeat the lesson to become more confident with the concept.

Notes on correcting assessments

When tallying assessment points, only count the number your student gets correct. Don't count the number of errors and subtract that from the given number of total points. As your student acquires their grammar knowledge, they may mark a part of speech that shouldn't be marked in a particular lesson. Do not count these misplaced marks as incorrect. This problem will resolve itself in time as they progress through the program.

For assessments with diagrams, you will notice that the diagrams in the solutions have check marks indicating what should be counted as a "point." Go through your student's diagram item by item and compare the checked items. If an item is in the correct place, make a checkmark. If it's in the wrong place, circle it so that your student can see where they made a mistake.

For modifiers, if they are attached to the correct word and diagrammed correctly, count them as correct even if the word they are modifying is in the wrong place.

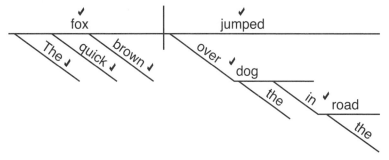

Example:
The quick brown fox jumped (over the dog) (in the road).
art adj adj n av pp art n pp art n

This diagram is worth seven points. Points are assigned for the subject (fox), verb (jumped), fox's modifiers (The, quick, and brown), the prepositional phrase attached to "jumped" (over the dog), and the prepositional phrase attached to "dog" (in the road). Notice that although the prepositional phrases have three words, they each only have one check mark and therefore are worth one point as a unit.

Now imagine your student diagrammed the sentence like this:

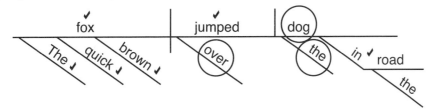

This diagram only loses one point. The prepositional phrase over the dog was only worth one point, so therefore it can only lose one point if it's incorrectly diagrammed. The prepositional phrase in the road is still correct and earns one point because it is correctly attached to *dog*.

Reinforcement Exercises

The student worktext includes 18 reinforcement exercises and answer keys that will keep your student's parsing, diagramming, and paraphrasing skills sharp. These exercises include material from a wide variety of books, poems, and stories. Students should complete, then correct, each exercise on their own. Assign one exercise every other week. If these skills are reinforced periodically, your student will be well-prepared when it's time to start Level 4.

Tips for Success

This course can be adapted to meet your student's needs.

- If your student is confident, consider allowing them to "test out" of a lesson. Have them look over the lesson notes and, if they feel ready, take the lesson assessment. If the student scores at least 80% correct on the assessment, skip to the next lesson. They will still get plenty of practice with the skipped concept.

- If a lesson feels overwhelming and your student needs to slow down a little, have them do the odd sentences in an exercise one day and the evens the next.

- Consider only asking your student to diagram half of the sentences in an exercise. If they understand the concept and can identify the word, phrase, or clause that is the focus of the lesson, they do not necessarily need to diagram every sentence.

- On the other hand, encourage students to diagram at least one or two sentences from each lesson. Diagramming creates a visual image of how parts of speech interact. Allow them to choose which sentences they would like to diagram.

- Remind your student that they should look at the lesson notes for help as they are completing the exercises and even the assessment.

Nouns, Adjectives, and Articles

Instructor Notes

Many students find this lesson relatively easy. This is a good way to build their confidence and ready them for subsequent lessons.

Analytical Grammar encourages students to ask themselves questions about parts of speech. By working through these questions systematically, they learn to analyze and identify the roles those parts of speech play in a sentence.

Rather than have your student silently read the examples in the lesson notes or exercises to themselves, ask them to verbalize what they are learning. Using the sentence in the Lesson Notes on the following page as an example, the student should read the sentence out loud and then talk through the answers to the following questions:

- What are the nouns in the sentence? Identifying nouns is the first step to identifying all of the other parts of speech in a sentence and the roles they play (*teenagers, song, Blue Suede Shoes*, which is a proper noun). At this point, we are only identifying the nouns, not their roles in the sentence.

    - Students may identify *Elvis Presley's* as a noun. By itself, it is a proper noun. However, the addition of *'s* makes it into an adjective describing "which (or whose) song?"

    - Students may want to identify *Shoes* as the noun, with *Blue and Suede* as modifiers. Point out that the entire title of the song is "*Blue Suede Shoes.*" Therefore, all of the words are part of the proper noun and should be included under the "wings," or the horizontal line drawn above all words in the noun.

- Next, help them to identify the articles and adjectives in the sentence. These two parts of speech only have one job: they will always modify nouns. They can be identified by taking each noun and turning it into a question using "which?" Any answers to that question will be modifiers, either adjectives or articles. Sometimes there will not be an answer, and that just means that the noun has no modifiers.

    - Which *teenagers*? *The* teenagers; *the* is an article.

    - Which *song*? *Elvis Presley's famous* song. As explained above, *Elvis Presley's* is an adjective. Sometimes called a proper adjective, these are identified with "wings," or a horizontal line drawn above the entire adjective. *Famous* is another adjective describing the song. They may identify *Elvis Presley's* as a noun, since it contains a proper noun. Point out the *'s* which makes it into a possessive adjective. It answers the question "which song?" or "whose song?"

    - Which *Blue Suede Shoes*? This proper noun doesn't have any additional modifiers.

Talking through the identification process will help students to not only identify parts of speech but also to begin to see what roles they are playing in a sentence.

When correcting a student's work, count how many words that should be marked have been identified correctly. If they have skipped several words that should be marked, review the lesson notes or video with them to be sure that they are comfortable identifying each part of speech. Remind them to use the notes as they complete the exercises. If your student has marked a word that that is not marked in the solutions, don't worry and don't mark it incorrect. As more parts of speech are introduced and mastered, your student will learn to differentiate between them.

Lesson 1: Nouns, Adjectives, and Articles

Nouns

A noun is a word that **names a person, place, thing, or idea**.

A **common noun** is a word that names an ordinary person, place, thing, or idea. Common nouns are never capitalized and consist of one word only.

Examples:

Persons:	teacher, man, girl
Places:	school, yard, city
Things:	bridge, carrot, building, day
Ideas:	anger, democracy, inspiration*

Nouns representing ideas are often called **abstract nouns.**

* Watch for the *-ion* ending—that's a strong indication that the word is a noun!

A proper noun is the **name** of a *specific* person, place, thing, or idea. Proper nouns are capitalized and may consist of more than one word. No matter how many words are in a proper noun, it still equals only one noun.

Examples:

Persons:	Ms. Jones, Nelson, George Washington Carver
Places:	Cranford High School; Anchorage, Alaska; Costa Rica
Things:	the Golden Gate Bridge; the NBA; Wrigley Field; April 1, 1492*
Ideas:	the Theory of Relativity, the Industrial Revolution

*All dates and years are proper nouns whether they are included in a date or by themselves. Think of them as the name for that specific day or year: not just any day, but June 30, specifically; not just any year, but 1986, in particular, for example.

Adjectives

Adjectives **modify,** or describe, **nouns and pronouns.** In English, they usually come in front of the noun they modify. Examples are *tall, silly, beautiful,* and *several.* For now, all of the adjectives you will be identifying will be next to the nouns they modify.

Watch out for **proper adjectives**! These are adjectives made out of proper nouns; for example, *England* is a proper noun, and *English* is the corresponding proper adjective. Just like the proper nouns they come from, they always begin with capital letters.

Articles

There are only three articles in English: *a, an,* and *the.* Articles always come in front of the nouns they modify, although not always directly in front of them. The article *a* is used in front of words that begin with a consonant sound (*a tree, a cat*), while *an* is used before words that begin with a vowel sound. This is decided by the word that is immediately after the article, not the noun; so, for example, *"**an** apple,"* but *"**a** big, red apple."*

Articles can be definite or indefinite. Imagine choosing an ice cream flavor from a line of tubs. You might say, "I want *the* one on the end," because that is the one you definitely want. If you are asked how you would like your ice cream served, you might say, "I would like it in *a* cone," because any old cone will do, as long as you have *the* flavor you asked for. *A* and *an* are indefinite articles because they are nonspecific. *The* is a definite article because it is specific.

When used in proper nouns or proper adjectives, articles are not capitalized unless they are the first word of the official name or title.

You've learned the names of three words: **noun**, **adjective**, and **article**. Words also do certain *jobs*. Adjectives and articles do the job of **modifying**, or giving more meaning to, nouns, so their job is that of **modifier**. That is the only job they do. Nouns can do five different jobs! These jobs will be discussed in future lessons, so for now, you just need to identify them as nouns.

Now it's time to put your new knowledge into practice! For the first few lessons, you will be *parsing* sentences. That means identifying the parts of speech in a sentence. Here's what to do:

Step 1: Find all the **nouns** in each sentence. Write *n* over the common nouns and *pn* over the proper nouns. If a proper noun is made up of more than one word, write *pn* in the middle and draw lines, or "wings," over all the words in the noun (see example).

                      n   *n*   ————pn————

Example: The teenagers loved Elvis Presley's famous song, "Blue Suede Shoes."

Notice that we didn't mark *Elvis Presley's* as a noun. Head to Step 2 to find out why!

Step 2: Find all of the **modifiers** (adjectives and articles) in the sentence. Do this by going back to each **noun** you identified and asking "which?" Any word located near the noun that answers this question is either an **article** or an **adjective**. Write *art* over the articles and *adj* over the adjectives. For our example, first ask yourself "which teenagers?" *The* teenagers. We know *the* is one of the three articles, so write *art* above. Then do the same for the remaining nouns.

Hint: Not all nouns have modifiers.

         art   *n*   ————*adj*————   *adj*   *n*   ————pn————

Example: The teenagers loved Elvis Presley's famous song, "Blue Suede Shoes."

When you ask yourself "which song?," the answer is *Elvis Presley's famous* song. The song is both *Elvis Presley's* and *famous*. Nouns can have many modifiers. What do you notice about *Elvis Presley's*? It includes a proper noun. It has been made into an adjective by adding *'s*, which shows that the song belongs to Elvis Presley. Adding *'s* is powerful—not only does it show possession, it makes a noun into an adjective! In this example, it makes a proper noun into a **proper adjective**. Mark these in the same way that you mark proper nouns, with "wings" over all of the words that are part of the proper adjective.

Nouns, Adjectives, and Articles: Exercise A

Directions

Step 1: Find all of the nouns. Write **n** over each common noun. Write **pn** over each proper noun. Use "wings" (—**pn**—) to include all of the words that are part of the proper noun if it's more than one word.

Step 2: Ask yourself "which?" about each noun. Write **adj** over each adjective and **art** over each article. Use wings to include all of the words that are part of a proper adjective. Look back at the lesson notes if you need help identifying any of the parts.

1) Even before the United States was a country, people played a game like baseball.

art ——pn—— art n n art n n

2) Baseball's rules were written down in 1845 by the Knickerbocker Baseball Club

adj n pn art —————pn—————

in New York City.

———pn———

3) The rules of the Knickerbocker Club's game have not changed much over the years.

art n art ————adj———— n art n

4) The American people couldn't get their fill of baseball!

art adj n adj n n

5) Talented players like Babe Ruth, Jackie Robinson, and Lou Gehrig became household names.

adj n ——pn—— ———pn——— ——pn—— adj n

Directions

Mark the nouns, adjectives, and articles like you did in the first section. Remember to use wings for proper nouns and proper adjectives that have more than one word. Look at the lesson notes if you need to.

<code>   adj   n   n   adj   n   art ———pn———</code>

1) Many kids wanted to play baseball like their heroes in the Major Leagues.

<code>   pn ———pn———   ———pn———   adj   n   n</code>

2) In 1939, Little League Baseball began in Williamsport, Pennsylvania, with three teams of kids.

<code>   *   ———pn———   n   adj   n   art   n</code>

3) Today, Little League Baseball is played by kids of all nationalities around the world.

* Your student may identify this adverb as a noun. If they do, don't worry, as this will sort itself out as they learn more parts of speech.

<code>   art ———pn———   adj   n   n   art   n</code>

4) The Little League World Series is held each year in countries across the globe.

<code>   art adj   n   adj   n   art   n   pn</code>

5) The winning teams from each region of the world go to Williamsport

<code>   art   adj   n</code>

for the championship tournament.

Short answer

6) Write the definition of a **noun**. Use a complete sentence.

A noun is a person, place, thing, or idea.

7) Which type of noun begins with a capital letter and may consist of more than one word?

A proper noun

Nouns, Adjectives, and Articles: Exercise B

Directions

Step 1: Find all of the nouns. Write **n** over each common noun. Write **pn** over each proper noun. Use "wings" **(—pn—)** to include all of the words that are part of the proper noun if it's more than one word.

Step 2: Ask yourself "which?" about each noun. Write **adj** over each adjective and **art** over each article. Use wings to include all of the words that are part of a proper adjective.

art adj adj n   ————pn———— ————pn————
1) On a cold, rainy day in December, 1891, Dr. James Naismith tried to think of

art n   adj adj n
a game to play with his gym class.

art n   *   pn
2) Because the class couldn't go outside, Naismith invented

art adj n   adj n   art   n
a new game for his students to play in the gymnasium.

Outside is an adverb; however, since adverbs haven't been introduced, your student may mark it as a noun naming a place. Don't be concerned if that happens. As more parts of speech are introduced and mastered, your student will learn to recognize the difference.

pn   art adj n   art adj   n   art n
3) Naismith hung a peach basket on the balcony's railing, and the students tried to throw

art adj n   art n
a socccer ball into the basket.

art adj   n   art n   art n   art n
4) The peach basket was a nuisance, because the students had to climb a ladder to

art n   adj n
retrieve the ball after each point.

adj adj n   n   art n   art adj adj n   art
5) Old soccer balls had laces that held a cover over an inflated rubber ball, causing the

n   adj   n
ball to bounce in unpredictable ways.

adj   *n*   *art* *n* *adj*   *n*   *art*   *n*

6) As more people came to the games, some spectators in the balcony began to

art *n*   *art*   *n*

interfere with the ball or the basket.

——*pn*——   *art*   *n*   *art* *adj*   *n*   *art* *adj* *n*   *n*

7) Dr. Naismith cut the bottom from the peach basket, approved a new ball without laces,

art   *n*   *art*   *n*

and added a backboard to protect the basket.

art   *adj*   *n*   *art*   *n*   *n*   *n*   *art*

8) The basket's backboard changed the game by adding rebounds and layups to the

adj   *n*

players' strategies.

pn ——*pn*——   *art* *adj*   *n*   *n*   *n*

9) In 1958, Coach Tony Hinkle made an orange ball that spectators and players

art *adj* *adj*   *n*

could see better than the old brown ones.

art   *n*   *n*   *art*   *adj* *n*

10) The game of basketball has changed a lot in the more than 130 years since

——*adj*——   *n*   *art* *adj* *adj*   *n*   ————*pn*————

Dr. Naismith's invention on a cold, rainy day in Springfield, Massachusetts.

Short answer

11) Write the definition of **adjective** in a complete sentence.

An adjective modifies or describes a noun.

Nouns, Adjectives, and Articles: Exercise C

Directions

Step 1: Find all of the nouns. Write **n** over each common noun. Write **pn** over each proper noun. Use "wings" (**—pn—**) to include all of the words that are part of the proper noun if it's more than one word.

Step 2: Ask yourself "which?" about each noun. Write **adj** over each adjective and **art** over each article. Use wings to include all of the words that are part of a proper adjective.

1) In the United States, football is a different sport than the game played in the rest

     of the world.

2) The first American football game was played on November 6, 1869, between Rutgers

     and Princeton, two college teams.

3) The game played that day looked a lot like soccer, because players were not allowed

     to pick up the round ball.

4) The twenty-five players on each team were allowed to kick or swat the

     ball with their feet, hands, and head.

5) The rules that developed into American football are actually from a game

     that began in Canada.

art   *adj*   *n*   *adj*   *n*   *adj*   *n*

6) The Canadian rules called for eleven players on each side and allowed

      n   *art*   *adj*   *n*

players to carry the oblong ball.

      ——*pn*———   *art*   ————*pn*————   *art* *adj*   *n*

7) Pudge Heffelfinger of the Allegheny Athletic Association was the first player paid to play

   art *adj*   *n*   *n*   ——*pn*——

the new game of football, in November, 1892.

      pn   *art* ————*pn*————   *art*   *n*   *adj*   *n*

8) In 1920, the National Football League was organized by a group of professional teams

      art   ————————*pn*————————

called the American Professional Football Association.

      art *adj* *adj*   *n*   *adj*   *n*   *adj*   *n*

9) The young NFL's rules said professional teams could not use college players

          n   *adj*   *n*

or steal players from other teams.

     art *adj* *adj*   *n*   *pn*   *art* *adj*   *n*

10) A rival football league began in 1960; however, the two leagues eventually merged

      adj   *pn*

into today's NFL.

Short answer

11) List the three **articles** in English. Use a complete sentence.

The articles are a, an, *and* the.

12) Where will you find the article in a sentence, in relationship to a noun?

The article will always be located before (or in front of) the noun it modifies.

Application & Enrichment

Paraphrasing Lesson 1

In each lesson, after Exercise C, you will find an Application & Enrichment activity. These mini-lessons introduce concepts and help you practice skills to improve your writing and communication.

Some Application & Enrichment exercises will ask you to **paraphrase** something. Paraphrasing is a skill you can use all throughout your school career and for the rest of your life: in book reports, writing essays and reports, and even telling a friend about a story you read or a movie you watched! When you paraphrase, you take what someone else has created and retell it in your own words.

For this exercise, you can change as many words and phrases as you want, but try to keep the basic structure of each sentence. Look for nouns and adjectives, and then find **synonyms** (words that mean the same thing) to replace them.

Here's an example from a famous poem called "Casey at the Bat" by Ernest Thayer:

> It looked extremely rocky for the Mudville nine that day;
>
> The score stood two to four, with but one inning left to play.
>
> So, when Cooney died at second and Burrows did the same,
>
> A pallor wreathed the features of the patrons of the game.

When you're paraphrasing, you need to read and understand what the original author is trying to say. In the first line, when the author says *It looked extremely rocky...*, do they mean that the ground where the game was played had literal rocks and stones lying around? No, of course not. They're saying that the team had a difficult task ahead of them. When you need to paraphrase, read the passage several times until you are sure that you understand what the author is saying.

Here's one possible paraphrase of the stanza above:

> Things looked rough for the Mudville baseball team that day.
>
> They were down two to four in the bottom of the ninth inning.
>
> So when Cooney was tagged out at second and so was Burrows,
>
> The fans' faces became deathly pale.

Here's another example from Mark Twain's great classic *Tom Sawyer*:

> "Hello, old chap, you got to work, hey?"
>
> Tom wheeled suddenly and said:
>
> "Why it's you, Ben, I warn't noticing."
>
> "Say—I'm going in a'swimming, I am. Don't you wish you could? But of course you'd druther work—wouldn't you? Course you would!"

Tom contemplated the boy a bit, and said:

"What do you call work?"

"Why, ain't *that* work?"

Tom resumed his whitewashing, and answered carelessly: "Well, maybe it is, and maybe it ain't. All I know is, it suits Tom Sawyer."

"Oh, come now, you don't mean to let on that you like it?"

The brush continued to move.

"Like it? Well, I don't see why I oughtn't to like it. Does a boy get a chance to whitewash a fence every day?"

That put the thing in a new light. Ben stopped nibbling his apple. Tom swept his brush daintily back and forth—stepped back to note the effect—added a touch here and there—criticized the effect again—Ben watching every move and getting more and more interested, more and more absorbed. Presently he said:

"Say, Tom, let *me* whitewash a little."

One possible paraphrase:

"Hiya, buddy, got chores to do, huh?"

Tom turned around quickly and said:

"Oh! It's you, Ben! Sorry, I wasn't paying attention."

"Hey, I'm going for a swim! Bet you wish you could go, too. But I can see you're really having a great time! SURE you are!"

Tom stared at Ben for a moment.

"Why shouldn't I be having a great time?"

"Are you trying to tell me that's fun?"

Tom went back to his painting and remarked casually:

"Maybe, maybe not. All I can tell you is I enjoy it."

"Oh please, Tom, don't try to tell me you're having fun!"

The paintbrush moved slowly back and forth.

"Why not? It's not every day a guy gets to whitewash a fence!"

This was a new way to look at the situation. Ben stopped chewing his apple. Tom took a swipe with his brush—stood back to look at the results—moved forward to make a couple more dabs—moved back to look again—Ben watching like a hawk, becoming increasingly fascinated, increasingly hooked. After a few moments he said:

"Hey, Tom? Can I try it for a little bit?"

Directions

Mark all of the common and proper nouns, adjectives, and articles in the following passage from the *Elmira Daily Advertiser* (Monday, July 4, 1887, p. 5). Then write a simple paraphrase of it by finding synonyms for as many nouns and adjectives as you can. You might have to look some words up in the dictionary if you don't know what they mean, and you may choose to use a thesaurus to find synonyms. Be as creative as you want, but try to keep as much of the original passage's meaning as possible.

————adj———— *n*   *art*   *n*   *adj*   *n*   *adj*   *n*

Mark Twain's effort to umpire a game of old-fashioned baseball on Saturday afternoon at

art ————*pn*————   *art*   *n*   *adj*   *n*

the Maple Avenue Park was not unmixed with an element of good-natured humbuggery.

Nouns, Adjectives, and Articles: Assessment

Here's your chance to show your skills by finding all of the nouns, adjectives, and articles in the following sentences. Then provide the definitions for the parts of speech you have been studying. Remember that you can look back at the notes if you are not sure.

Directions

Write **n** over the common nouns, **pn** over the proper nouns (don't forget the "wings," if necessary), **adj** over the adjectives, and **art** over the articles.

Each correctly identified part of speech is worth one point.

___
11
1) The game of football, or soccer, is played by more people around the world than

any other sport.
<small>adj adj n</small>

___
12
2) Many people believe the game began to be called *soccer* in the United States, but the
<small>adj n art n n art ——pn—— art</small>

nickname originated in England in the 1880s.
<small>n pn art pn</small>

___
10
3) Before that time, *football* referred to any kind of game in which a ball was kicked
<small>adj n n adj n n art n</small>

to score a goal.
<small>art n</small>

___
13
4) Association football got its name when England's Football Association wrote down a set
<small>adj n adj n adj ——pn—— art n</small>

of rules for one type of football game.
<small>n adj n adj n</small>

___
8
5) To differentiate among the many games called *football*, this game was officially called
<small>art adj n n adj n</small>

association football.
<small>adj n</small>

_____
14

         adj   *adj*   *n*   *adj* *adj*   *n*   *adj*   *n*

6) English college students liked to play two main games: rugby football, named after

   art *adj*   *adj*   *n*   *adj*   *n*

a British boarding school, and association football.

_____
12

   art   *n*   *adj* *adj* *adj*   *n*   *art*   *adj*   *n*   *n*

7) The students gave their two favorite games the shortened nicknames of "rugger" and

          n   *n*

"asoccer," which was shortened again to "soccer."

_____
9

            pn   *n*   *art*   *n*   *art*   *n*   *art*

8) In England, "soccer" was never more than a nickname, and the game took over the

      n   *n*

name of "football."

_____
12

       art ——*pn*——   *pn*   *pn*   *n*   *adj* *adj*

9) In the United States, Canada, and Australia, people already played their own

   adj   *n*   *adj*   *n*   *n*

popular versions of different games called "football."

_____
11

          n   *n*   *adj*   *n*   *adj*   *n*   *adj* *n*

10) To avoid confusion, players of association football in these countries called their sport

   n   *art*   *n*

"soccer," and the name stuck.

=====
112

Short answer

___**11)** Define **noun**:

1   *A noun is the name of a person, place, thing, or idea.*

___**12)** Define **adjective**:

1   *An adjective modifies a noun or pronoun.*

___**13)** Which kind of noun always begins with a lowercase letter and consists of only one word?

1   *A common noun*

___**14)** List the three articles in the English language:

3   *The articles are* a, an, *and* the.

$$\overline{\overline{}}$$
6

$$\overline{\overline{}}\ Total\ Points \quad \frac{94}{118} = 80\%$$
118

Lesson 2
Pronouns

Instructor Notes

Pronouns play an important role in our language, and they fall into different categories that fill different jobs in English. While it is not necessary for students to memorize the lists provided, it is important that they are very familiar with these words. Remind them to refer to their lesson notes and look at the lists if they are not sure whether a word is a pronoun. For this lesson, they do not need to identify different kinds or cases of pronouns. It is enough that they can recognize a pronoun when they see one.

Students should learn to use the word **antecedent** correctly. Rather than saying, "*it* stands for *bird*," for example, students should say, "*It* is a pronoun, and the antecedent of *it* is *bird*." This word becomes important in ensuring agreement between the antecedent and pronoun in the usage lessons in Level 5, so students should become comfortable with it now.

While they are verbalizing the steps, students should first identify the nouns in the sentence, then the adjectives and articles, then the pronouns. Since some pronouns can act as adjectives, identifying pronouns after the other parts of speech will help to avoid confusion. Pronouns acting as adjectives will have already been labeled prior to identifying the pronouns in the sentence. Focus on correct identification of the parts of speech that should be marked, and don't worry if your student marks words that should not be. This will sort itself out as new parts of speech are introduced and mastered.

A Tip for Instructors

If your student confidently completes Exercise A independently and without error, you may skip Exercises B and C and give them the option of taking the assessment early. If they score at least an 80% on the assessment, they are ready to move on. Decide with your student whether to jump into the next lesson immediately, or take a short break and wait for the following Monday. Either way, your student should still complete that lesson's Application & Enrichment activity before moving on.

Lesson 2: Pronouns

A **pronoun** is a word that takes the place of one or more nouns with their modifiers. A pronoun can do anything a noun can do. Sometimes it even has its own modifiers! (These are usually adjectives; you won't often find a pronoun with an article as a modifier.) Here are a couple of definitions that will help us to talk about pronouns.

Antecedents

An **antecedent** is the noun or nouns that the pronoun stands for. Some pronouns don't have stated antecedents, because the antecedents are understood from **context**. Sometimes you will find the antecedent in a previous sentence.

Context

For our purposes, **context** is the setting or meaning of a word, sentence, or paragraph. When we are reading, we consider all words in their context, whether they are familiar or unfamiliar, by looking at their relationship to other words around them. If the words are unfamiliar, or, as with a pronoun, they are standing in for another word, we look for clues from the surrounding text to figure out what the word means. If a reader isn't able to figure out the antecedent of a pronoun from context, the sentence probably should be rewritten!

      pn   *pro*

Example: Jasmine said she was tired.   *The word* **Jasmine** *is the* **antecedent** *for* **she.**

You don't need to memorize the following lists of pronouns, but you do need to read these lists and definitions carefully to be sure you can recognize a pronoun when you see one. You also should be aware that different kinds of pronouns are used in different situations. We'll learn more about those situations later. Right now, just focus on identifying them.

There are five main categories of pronouns in the English language.

Personal Pronouns

These pronouns occur in four "cases." Don't worry about when these cases are used yet. Just become familiar with the pronouns, enough so that you can recognize them when you see them. Personal pronouns should have clear antecedents, or they can cause confusion.

	Subjective	Objective	Possessive	Reflexive/Intensive*
Singular	I	me	mine	myself
	you	you	yours	yourself/yourselves
	he	him	his*	himself
	she	her*	hers	herself
	it	it	its	itself
Plural	we	us	ours	ourselves
	they†	them†	theirs†	themselves†

†The pronouns on the last row—*they, them, theirs, and themselves*—are also used as gender-neutral singular pronouns when the antecedent's gender is unknown or not relevant to the context of the sentence. For example, instead of saying, "*He* or *she* should go to the bus stop after school," we should say, "*They* should go to the bus stop after school."

Indefinite Pronouns

Indefinite pronouns are those with unknown or nonspecific antecedents. We don't know what noun these pronouns are replacing. "Someone left the water running." "Does anyone really like pineapple on pizza?" "Several have yellow flowers." It's not the quantity that's indefinite (for example, "somebody" always takes the singular form of the verb—we'll get to that later!); it's the antecedent. So when we hear, "He ate three of them!" we are unsure what he ate—cheeseburgers? apples? entire pizzas?—but we know there were three. In this example, then, *three* is an indefinite pronoun.

Singular	Plural	Either
another*	both*	all*
anybody	few*	any*
anyone	many*	more*
anything	most*	none
each*	others	some*
either*	several*	
everybody	two*, three*, etc. (all cardinal numbers can be indefinite pronouns)	

The following are only **singular** and have no plural:

everyone	no one	other*
everything	nobody	somebody
much	nothing	someone
neither	one*	something

Demonstrative Pronouns

Think of pointing at something in the store display case: "What do you want?" "I want *that*." Demonstrative pronouns point something out or set it apart. These pronouns usually do not have antecedents.

Singular	Plural
that*	those*
this*	these*

Interrogative Pronouns

Have you ever heard of someone being *interrogated*? That's when someone is asked a lot of questions, usually in a formal investigation. That's where the name *interrogative pronouns* comes from—these are pronouns that are used to ask questions. They usually come in cases like the personal pronouns. These pronouns don't have antecedents and can be singular or plural.

Subjective	Objective	Possessive	No Case
who	whom	whose*	which, what
whoever	whomever	whosever*	whichever, whatever

Relative Pronouns

Relative pronouns, along with the adjective clauses they introduce, answer the questions "Who?" "What?" "Which?" about a noun. They are words you already know, and we will talk about them in Level 4 when we learn about adjective clauses. These are all the relative pronouns:

who/whom	what	which	that*

*Remember that we said that parts of speech have one name but can have many jobs? Note that several of the pronouns listed have asterisks next to them. The pronouns with the asterisks can act as adjectives at times. That's why it's best to follow the suggested order when you are parsing sentences. If you have already marked one of these words as an adjective in the sentence (if it answers the question "which?"), then it isn't acting as a pronoun in the sentence. Look at this example:

                pn   pro adj   n
Example: Jack loaned me his book.

*Note that **his** is being used as an adjective in this sentence: Which book? **His** book.*

                pn   art   n   pro
Example: Jack said the book was his.

*Note that **his** is being used as a pronoun in this sentence. Its **antecedent** is "Jack's book."*

Many words that are similar to some of the pronouns you've just studied (such as *my, your, our, their*) can **only** be used as adjectives. That's why they aren't listed with the personal pronouns. Some grammar books call these words "possessive pronouns." In this program, however, we will simply call them adjectives, since they are doing an adjective's job.

Pronouns: Exercise A

Directions

In this exercise, the focus is on personal pronouns. Personal pronouns have antecedents, although they may not be found in the same sentence. Look back a sentence or two, if needed. Pronouns are easier to identify if you find all of the nouns and their modifiers first.

Step 1: Find all of the nouns. Write *n* over each common noun and *pn* over each proper noun. (Don't forget the "wings," if necessary!)

Step 2: Ask yourself "which?" about each noun. Write *adj* over each adjective and *art* over each article. Use "wings" to include all of the words that are part of a proper adjective. Be on the lookout for pronouns that are doing the adjective job!

Step 3: Find all of the personal pronouns and write *pro* over each one. Below each sentence, write each pronoun and its antecedent.

Example:

     pn   *art adj n* *pro*   *pro*

 1) David aimed at the distant target, but he just couldn't hit it.

    he = David   it = target

   pro *art* *n* *pro*   *art* *n*   *pro*   * *pro* *pn*

2) "I know the reason you missed the target, but do you know what it is, David?"

       pn

asked Marina.

  I = Marina *you, you = David* *it = reason*

 What is not parsed in this activity because it is an interrogative pronoun; the focus of this activity is personal pronouns. If your student marks what *but can't find the antecedent, show them in the notes that it is an interrogative pronoun and doesn't have one.*

   pn   *pn*   *pro* *adj n* * *pro*

3) David looked at Marina, but he had no idea what she meant.

  he = David *she = Marina*

   pn *pn adj* *n* *pn*   *adj* *n* *pro*

4) Jacob and Tom, both friends of David, were puzzled by her question themselves.

  themselves = Jacob and Tom

   pn   *pro*   *pro art* *n*   *adj adj* *n*

5) David muttered to himself, "Seems to me the problem must be this old slingshot."

  himself, me = David

             pn   *adj*   *n*   *pro*   *pro*   *pro*

6) When Marina heard his response, she chuckled to herself about it.

    she, herself = Marina   *it = response*

    pro   *pn*   *pro*   *pro*   *art*   *n*   *pro*   *pro*

7) She said to David, "If you think you can hit the target, you will hit it."

    She = Marina   *you, you, you = David*   *it = target*

    pro   *   *art*   *adj*   *n*   *art* *adj*   *n*

8) She knew that just thinking a positive thought could have a large impact on whether

    art   *n*   *pro*

he hit the target or missed it.

    She = Marina   *he = David*   *it = target*

    * That *is not parsed in this activity because it is a relative pronoun; the focus of this activity is personal pronouns. If your student marks* that *but can't find the antecedent, show them in the notes that it is a relative pronoun and doesn't have one.*

    pn   *pro*   *pro*   *art* *n*   *pro*

9) David realized she was right and wished he had thought of the idea himself!

    she = Marina   *he, himself = David*

    pn   *adj* *adj*   *n*   *art*   *n*   *art* *n*

10) David raised his loaded slingshot, thought about the bullseye, and placed a marble

    art   *n*   *pro*

in the center of it.

    it = bullseye

Fill in the blank

11) A pronoun is a word which takes the place of a _____.

    noun

Pronouns: Exercise B

Directions

In this exercise, the focus is on demonstrative and interrogative pronouns, although it also includes some personal pronouns. Since demonstrative and interrogative pronouns don't usually have antecedents, you won't have to look for them.

Step 1: Find all of the nouns. Write *n* over each common noun and *pn* over each proper noun. (Don't forget the "wings," if necessary!)

Step 2: Ask yourself "which?" about each noun. Write *adj* over each adjective and *art* over each article. Use "wings" to include all of the words that are part of a proper adjective.

Step 3: Find all of the pronouns and write *pro* over each one. Remember to check the list if you're not sure if a word is a pronoun. (Be on the lookout for pronouns that are doing the adjective job! They are probably already marked as adjectives.)

1)
		art	adj	adj	n	pro		art	n	pro
——pn——										

Johnny Carson was a late-night television host, but he once made a joke that caused

adj	n		pro

some trouble for him.

2)
pro	pro		pro		art	n		adj	n	adj	n

What he claimed was that there was a shortage of paper towels in this country.

3)
pro			pro	art	n		adj	n		pro

He went on to describe what the consequences of this shortage might be, which alarmed

adj	n	pro		pro

many people who listened to him.

4)
art	n		adj	n	pro	n			adj	n

The implication of this joke was that people had better stock up on paper towels quickly

art	n

or face the consequences.

5)
pro		art	adj	n	pro	pro		art	n	adj	n

This was a humorous skit to those who knew a shortage of paper towels did not exist.

       n   *art adj*   *n*   *pro*

6) Within days, however, a real shortage developed, which was surprising!

    pro   *pro*   *art adj*   *n*   *pro*

7) Those who did not realize there was not a real shortage went out and bought up all of

 art adj   *n*   *pro*

the paper towels they could find.

   pro   *art adj*   *n*   *pro*   *n*   *pro*

8) This disrupted the normal distribution, which created shortages for whoever really needed

 adj   *n*

paper towels.

   pro   *art*   *n*   *pro*   *adj*   *n*

9) Whoever believed the shortage to be true acted on it and, by their actions, caused

 art   *n*

the belief to become true.

   pro   *adj*   *n*   *art* *adj*   *n*   *pro*

10) This is another example of a self-fulfilling prophecy which came about because of

 pro   *n*

what people thought.

Fill in the blank

11) A pronoun is a word which _____ of a noun.

    takes the place

12) A noun is the name of _____.

    a person, place, thing, or idea

13) An adjective _____.

    modifies or describes a noun

14) An antecedent is _____.

    the noun the pronoun takes the place of

Pronouns: Exercise C

Directions

This exercise is designed to give you practice with the indefinite pronouns, but all of the other pronouns are included, too. Remember to refer to your notes if you need help.

Step 1: Find all of the nouns. Write **n** over each common noun. Write **pn** over each proper noun. Use wings to include all of the words that are part of a proper noun, if necessary.

Step 2: Ask yourself "which?" about each noun. Write **adj** over each adjective and **art** over each article. Use wings to include all of the words that are part of a proper adjective.

Step 3: Find all of the pronouns and write **pro** over each of them. Be careful—there is one pronoun that needs wings!

1) Many who are successful at what they do in life have a positive mental attitude.
      pro   pro   *pro   pro*   *n*   *art adj   adj   n*

2) Everyone knows that students in our school have positive and creative attitudes.
      pro   *pro   n   adj   n   adj   adj   n*

3) All of us believe our school is the best, and, because we think it is the best, we act
      pro   pro   adj   n   art   n   pro   pro   art n   pro

    in ways that make it the best.
      n   pro   pro art   n

4) Everyone who visits our school is impressed by the friendly, helpful students and faculty.
      pro   pro   adj   n   art   adj   adj   n   n

5) All of us work to keep our halls and cafeteria clean so everyone can enjoy them
      pro   pro   adj   n   n   pro   pro

    as much as we do.
               pro   pro

pro   pro   pro   adj   n   pro

6) When we see someone who is careless about our school, we remain positive and do

pro   pro   art   n

whatever we can to correct the problem.

pro   n   adj adj   n   —pro—   pro

7) Hundreds of people watch our sports teams, but no one has ever accused us of

adj   n

poor sportsmanship.

pro   pro   art   n   n   n   art   n   art   n

8) Anyone who has a question or problem can always get help from a teacher, a counselor,

art   n

or a principal.

pro   pro   adj n   pro   adj n   art n

9) We cannot manage everything at one time, so we manage one thing at a time.

pro   pro   pro   pro   pro

10) Often, if someone believes they can do something, they will do it!

Fill in the blank

11) A pronoun _____.

     takes the place of a noun

12) The three articles are _____.

     a, an, *and* the

Application & Enrichment

Paraphrasing Activity 2

We learned a little about paraphrasing in the Application & Enrichment activity in Lesson 1. It is an essential skill to be able to process information and put it into your own words, because using other writers' words is called **plagiarism**. Plagiarism is taking someone else's words or ideas and presenting them as your own. This can include just changing words while keeping the structure of the sentence. That's why it is so important to read and read and read a passage until you understand it and can put it into your own words. Look at the following example from Mark Twain's *A Connecticut Yankee in King Arthur's Court*:

> "It was in Warwick Castle that I came across the curious stranger whom I am going to talk about. He attracted me by three things: his candid simplicity, his marvelous familiarity with ancient armor, and the restfulness of his company—for he did all the talking. We fell together, as modest people will, in the tail of the herd that was being shown through, and he at once began to say things which interested me."

Here is a "paraphrase" that is actually plagiarism:

> It was in Warwick Castle that I met the odd fellow whom I am going to tell you about. He fascinated me by three characteristics: his honest directness, his amazing acquaintance with old armor, and the peacefulness of his presence—for he did all the speaking. We ended up together, as humble folk will, at the end of the line that was being taken on the tour, and he immediately started to speak of things that intrigued me.

The sentences are all the same; they just have a few different words! Now look at this paraphrase of the same passage:

> I met the unusual man that I want to tell you about while I was visiting Warwick Castle. Both of us, not being the pushy type, were hanging to the back of the tour group when he began to give interesting commentary on what we were seeing. I was fascinated with his wealth of knowledge about ancient armor, and his straightforwardness and pleasantness made me like him right away, even though I couldn't get a word in.

It is clearly the same passage, but the sentence structure, word choice, and even the sequence that the information is presented in is different from the original.

Directions

In Lesson 1's Application & Enrichment, you replaced the adjectives and nouns in the following sentence to make it different. Mark all of the nouns (**n**), adjectives (**adj**), and articles (**art**) again, and mark any pronouns (**pro**), too. Next, reread the sentence until you are sure you know what it says. Finally, cover the sentence and rewrite it in your own words. You can change words, sentence structure, or anything else you would like, as long as you try to provide the same information in your rewritten sentence as is given in the original.

——adj——   n   art   n   adj   n   adj   n

Mark Twain's effort to umpire a game of old-fashioned baseball on Saturday afternoon at

art   ——pn——   art   n   adj   n

the Maple Avenue Park was not unmixed with an element of good-natured humbuggery.

Pronouns: Assessment

Directions

Mark all of the nouns (*n*), proper nouns (*pn*), adjectives (*adj*), articles (*art*), and pronouns (*pro*). Be sure to use wings, if necessary. Remember that you can look at the notes pages if you need help.

        pn   *pro* *pn*   *pro*   *pro*   *pro*   *pro*

$\frac{}{8}$ **1)** Sofia once said to me, "Aya, if you think something is true, even if it isn't, you can

           pro

make it become true."

      adj   *n*   *adj*   *n*   *pro*   *pro*

$\frac{}{7}$ **2)** Many people have accomplished impossible things simply because they thought they

           pro

could do them.

      n   *n*   *adj*   *n*   *pro*   *adj*   *n*   *pro*

$\frac{}{9}$ **3)** Humans love stories of everyday people who do impossible things because they

          pro

believe in themselves.

    pro *art* *adj*   *n*   *n*   *n* *art* *adj* *n*   *adj* *n*

$\frac{}{15}$ **4)** This is a popular theme of folktales and fables: the brave hero or lucky fool

    pro   *art*   *adj*   *n*

who accomplishes an impossible task.

      pro   *pro* *art* *n*   *   *pro*

$\frac{}{8}$ **5)** Because they did not believe that the task was impossible, they thought creatively

        art *n*   *pro*

and found a way to do it.

                n   *   *n*   *pro*   *adj*   *n*

$\frac{\quad}{8}$ **6)** Folktales are full of characters who are given impossible tasks to complete and

            pro   *pro*   *pro*

who refuse to believe they can't do them.

         ——*pn*——   *pro* *pro*   *art*   *n*

$\frac{\quad}{9}$ **7)** King Arthur didn't know that he shouldn't have been able to pull the sword from

    art   *n*   *pro*   *pro*

the stone, so he tried and he succeeded.

      adj   *n*   *adj*   *n*   *adj*   *n*   *pro*   *adj*   *n*

$\frac{\quad}{12}$ **8)** Greek mythology has many stories of human heroes who were given impossible tasks

         pro   *pro*   *pro*

by those who hoped they would fail.

      adj   *n*   *adj*   *n*   *pro*   *art* *n*   *n*   *n*

$\frac{\quad}{13}$ **9)** Japanese folklore tells of two sisters who found a way to wrap fire and wind

         n   *pro*   *adj*   *n*

in paper so they could earn their freedom.

      adj   *n*   *art*   *n*   *n*   *adj*   *n*   *adj*   *n*   *pro*

$\frac{\quad}{15}$ **10)** Every country in the world has stories of brave heroes and lucky fools who succeed

      adj   *n*   *pro*   *   *pro*   *pro*

at impossible tasks because they are positive they can do it!

$\overline{\overline{}}$
104

* **Note:** *Three words are marked with asterisks. These words are adjectives, but they are predicate adjectives, which your student will not learn for several lessons. If your student identifies these words as adjectives, give them a bonus point! They are paying very close attention to the jobs that words are doing in the sentence. If they do not recognize them as adjectives, do not count them incorrect. Only adjectives that are placed before the noun are counted as part of the total score.*

Fill in the blank

___11) A noun is the name of _____ .

   1   *a person, place, thing, or idea*

___12) A proper noun always begins with _____ .

   1   *a capital letter*

___12) A _____ noun can only consist of one word, but a

   2   _____ noun can be more than one word.

            common, proper

___13) The articles are _____ .

   3   *a, an, and the*

___14) An adjective modifies _____ and _____ .

   2   *nouns, pronouns*

___15) A pronoun _____ .

   1   *takes the place of a noun*

___15) A pronoun _____ .

   1   *takes the place of a noun*

___16) An antecedent is _____ .

   1   *the noun the pronoun stands for*

   ====

   11

=== *Total Points* $\dfrac{92}{115} = 80\%$

115

Lesson 3
Prepositional Phrases

Instructor Notes

Students will add another step to their verbalizing in this lesson. They should continue to identify all of the parts of speech that they have already studied, then add, "_____ is a preposition, and the prepositional phrase is _____."

This lesson also introduces the first baby steps toward sentence diagramming. Provide your student with all of the help they need as they are beginning to learn this new skill. It is a valuable tool that they can use to visualize the relationships among parts of speech until the relationships are solidly established in their minds.

Lesson 3: Prepositional Phrases

A preposition is a word used to show the relationship between two nouns.

Example: The package <u>under</u> the tree is mine. (under is the preposition)

The package <u>in</u> the tree is mine. (in is the preposition)

The package <u>near</u> the tree is mine. (near is the preposition)

Notice how the relationship between the package and the tree changes when the preposition is changed. Changing the preposition moves the package!

How to find a preposition

Think: anywhere a mouse can go! Most prepositions will fit into the following little sentence:

"The mouse goes _____ the box (or boxes)."

This handy little sentence will identify the majority of prepositions. Try it with the ones used in the example sentences above. They fit, don't they? If you can use a word in this sentence that describes where the mouse is in relation to the box, you know it could be a preposition.

But remember that we said "most"? There are some prepositions that don't fit. There are nine very common ones that we use all the time in our language, which may seem like a lot to remember. Here's a little memory aid: you may not be able to remember all nine, BUT AL DOES!

B = but (but me)	**A** = as (as a fox)	**D** = during (during recess)
U = until (until lunch)	**L** = like (like a dog)	**O** = of (of your homework)
T = than (than the others)		**E** = except (except that one)
		S = since (since breakfast)

Phrases
A phrase is a group of words that work together as a unit to express a concept.

A preposition is **not** a preposition unless it's in a prepositional phrase. A word may fit into the mouse-box sentence and look like a preposition, but the job it's doing in the sentence means that it's not acting as a preposition at the time. In that case, the word is almost always an **adverb** (which we will learn about in Lesson 5). Don't worry, there aren't any trick questions about "preposition or adverb?" in this lesson!

Practice

Use the mouse-box sentence or "BUT AL DOES" to test each word. Mark the prepositions with an *X*.

X	between		what
X	but	*X*	above
X	about		when
	then	*X*	beyond
	and	*X*	without

To find a prepositional phrase, you say the preposition and ask, "what?" You are looking for a noun or pronoun that answers that question. That noun or pronoun is called the **object of the preposition**.

Example:

art   n   pp art   n

The dog barked (at the cat).

Note: When you're parsing, put parentheses around the whole prepositional phrase.

We know that *at* is a preposition, because it fits into the mouse-box sentence (a little awkwardly, but it fits). So we ask the question, "*at* what?" The answer is "*cat*" (strip out all the modifiers so you have just the noun; *the* isn't part of the answer). *Cat* is the object of the preposition.

Each prepositional phrase will:

- begin with a preposition

- end with a noun or pronoun

- contain only prepositions, nouns, and modifiers

If there are any other words between the preposition and its object, they are modifiers (articles or adjectives) of the object. **No other kinds of words can be in a prepositional phrase.**

In the first example of this lesson, the prepositional phrases are *under the tree*, *in the tree*, and *near the tree*. **Tree** is the object of the preposition in all three phrases.

Because a phrase is a unit, prepositional phrases have a job to do as a unit: **they are always modifiers.** If a phrase is not acting as a modifier, it can't be a prepositional phrase.

Look at these sentences:

I ate my lunch **before recess**.

(The prepositional phrase is **before recess**; *before* is a preposition and *recess* is the object of the preposition.)

I ate my lunch **before.**

(*Before* isn't acting as a preposition in this sentence because there's no object. If you ask, "before what?", there's no answer.)

I ate my lunch **before I saw you.**

(Again, *before* isn't acting as a preposition. If you ask, "before what?", the answer would be "before I saw you." That's not a prepositional phrase, because there are other words besides nouns/pronouns and modifiers. A verb will never be in a prepositional phrase.)

Practice

Put parentheses around the prepositional phrases in these sentences. Remember that a prepositional phrase must have a preposition and a noun or pronoun (plus any modifiers of the noun/pronoun). It must also answer the question "**(preposition)** what?"

1) The movie was exciting, like the reviews said.

pp art   n

2) The movie was exciting, (like the book).

3) I like exciting movies.

pp   art adj   n

4) Our exam was less difficult (than the last one).

5) Our exam was less difficult than we thought it would be.

6) I cannot marry you, for I love another.

pp   adj   n

7) I cannot marry you (for two reasons).

Now, parse the prepositional phrases you have identified, marking prepositions (**pp**), nouns (**n**), pronouns (**pro**), and modifiers—articles (**art**) and adjectives (**adj**). All of the words in a prepositional phrase must be one of these parts of speech. Are there any words within the parentheses that can't be marked as one of these parts of speech? If there are, it is not a prepositional phrase, and the word that looks like a preposition is not doing a preposition's job in the sentence.

Diagramming

Sentence diagramming is a tool we use, much like drawing pictures. We use diagrams to make it easier to see concepts that might be difficult to understand. Diagrams consist of three types of lines:

Horizontal	Vertical	Diagonal
──	│	╲

The basic diagram of a prepositional phrase looks like this:

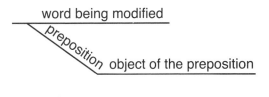

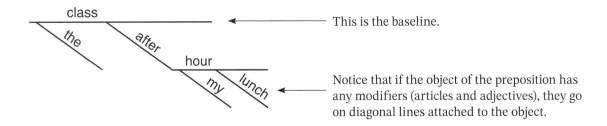

A few prepositions consist of more than one word. They are *because of, on account of, in spite of, regardless of, according to, instead of, contrary to,* and *out of.* If you find one of these prepositions, label it **pp** and use wings to include all of the words (like you do with proper nouns).

Prepositional Phrases: Exercise A

Directions

Step 1: Find all of the nouns. Write **n** over each common noun. Write **pn** over each proper noun. Use wings to include all of the words that are part of a proper noun, if necessary.

Step 2: Ask yourself, "which?" about each noun. Write **adj** over each adjective and **art** over each article. Use wings to include all of the words that are part of a proper adjective.

Step 3: Find all of the pronouns and write **pro** over each of them.

Step 4: Find all of the prepositions and write **pp** over them. Put parentheses around all prepositional phrases, being sure to include the preposition (**pp**), the object (**n**, **pn**, or **pro**), and any modifiers of the object.

Once you have parsed the sentence, use a separate sheet of paper to diagram the prepositional phrases in each sentence. The first sentence has been done for you as an example. Don't worry about what word the phrase is modifying yet; just draw a blank baseline.

Some of the words in the sentences have been underlined. After you finish parsing and diagramming, you will be asked a question about these words.

Diagramming solutions are found at the end of this book.

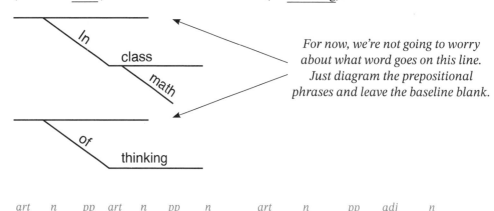

                   pp adj   n   pro   art adj   n   pp   n

Example: **1)**   (In math <u>class</u>,) we use a certain method (of <u>thinking</u>).

For now, we're not going to worry about what word goes on this line. Just diagram the prepositional phrases and leave the baseline blank.

    n   art   n   pp art n   pp   n   art   n   pp adj   n

2)   People think a person (with a <u>mind</u>) (for <u>math</u>) has an advantage (over other <u>people</u>).

      adj   n   n   pp   adj   n

3)   Such people appear to learn concepts (about mathematical <u>principles</u>) easily.

     pro   n   pp   n

4)   They solve problems (in <u>math</u>) quickly.

     adj   n   pp adj   n   n   pp   n

5)   Emotional blocks (in your <u>mind</u>) can prevent success (in <u>math</u>).

 art n   pp adj   n   pp art   n   pro art adj   n   pp   n

6) A belief (in your ability) (as a mathematician) gives you a better chance (at success).

    art   n   pp   adj   n   pp adj   n

7) The "gift" (of mathematical ability) exists (in all people).

    art n pp   n   pp   adj   n   art n pp   n

8) A lack (of success) (with certain problems) seldom indicates a lack (of ability).

    pp   n   pro   pp art n pp   n   pp   n

9) (In school,) we look (for the key) (to success) (in mathematics).

    ——pp——   *adj   n   pp   n   pp   n   pro   adj   n*

10) (Instead of "special" brains) (with ability) (in math), we need more confidence

    pp adj adj   n

(in our own ability)!

Short answer

11) All the underlined words in this exercise are doing the same job. Look at your notes and write what that job is.

_____

object of the preposition

Prepositional Phrases: Exercise B

Directions

Step 1: Find all of the nouns. Write **n** over each common noun. Write **pn** over each proper noun. Use wings to include all of the words that are part of a proper noun, if necessary.

Step 2: Ask yourself "which?" about each noun. Write **adj** over each adjective and **art** over each article. Use wings to include all of the words that are part of a proper adjective.

Step 3: Find all of the pronouns and write **pro** over each of them.

Step 4: Find all of the prepositions and write **pp** over them. Put parentheses around each prepositional phrase.

Once you have parsed the sentence, use a separate sheet of paper to diagram the prepositional phrases in each sentence.

Some of the words in the sentences have been underlined. After you finish parsing and diagramming, you will be asked a question about each of these words.

Diagramming solutions are found at the end of this book.

1) Would you be surprised to learn that calculators were used (before the discovery) (of electricity)?

2) There is an ancient calculating tool called an abacus that has been used (for thousands)

(of years)!

3) (In countries) (in the Near East), abacuses have been used (for business) (for many centuries).

4) Abacuses are still used today (in many cultures).

5) Skilled users (of an abacus) can calculate (at speeds) similar to those (of calculator users).

6) What we picture (as an abacus) is made (of movable beads) (on rods)

(in a rectangular frame).

pro   adj   adj   n   pp   n

7) There are <u>many</u> different types (of abacuses).

pro   n   ——pp——   n   n   ——pp——   n

8) Some have strings (instead of wires) and knots (instead of beads).

pro   n   pp   n   pp   adj   n   pro   pp   n   pp   n

9) Others have trays (with sections) (for small <u>stones</u>) that are moved (from place) (to place).

art   adj   n   pp   n   adj   n   pro   art adj   n   pp   n

10) The <u>Chinese</u> word (for abacus) means "counting tray," and that is a good name (for it)!

Directions

The underlined words in these sentences are doing one of two jobs. Choose your answer from the jobs below and write what job each underlined word is doing.

           modifier   ***object of the preposition***

Sentence #	Word	Job
1	electricity	*object of the preposition*
2	calculating	*modifier*
4	cultures	*object of the preposition*
5	abacus	*object of the preposition*
7	many	*modifier*
9	stones	*object of the preposition*
10	Chinese	*modifier*

Prepositional Phrases: Exercise C

Directions

Parse the sentences by marking all of the nouns (**n**), proper nouns (**pn**), adjectives (**adj**), articles (**art**), pronouns (**pro**), and prepositions (**pp**). Put parentheses around each prepositional phrase.

Once you have parsed the sentence, use a separate sheet of paper to diagram the prepositional phrases.

Some of the words in the sentences have been underlined. After you finish parsing and diagramming, you will be asked a question about these words.

Diagramming solutions are found at the end of this book.

    ——pp——   *adj*   *n*   *pro*   *adj*   *n*   *pp*   *adj*   *n*

1) (Contrary to popular belief), you use your imagination (in math class).

         pp   *art*   *n*   *pp*   *n*   *art*   *n*   *pp*   *n*   *pp*   *art*

2) Early (in the history) (of mathematics), the imagination (of <u>mathematicians</u>) led (to the

       n   *pp*   *adj*   *adj*   *adj*   *n*

discovery) (of each new mathematical theorem).

      art   *n*   *pp*   *adj*   *n*   *art*   *n*   *pp*   *adj*   *adj*   *n*

3) The act (of mathematical creation) involves the use (of all <u>one's</u> abilities).

      pp   *adj*   *n*   *art*   *n*   *pp*   *n*   *art*   *n*   *pp*   *art*   *adj*   *n*

4) (In most cases), the gift (of logic) plays only a part (in the mathematical process).

      pp   *adj*   *n*   *pp*   *n*   *n*   *pp*   *n*   *art*   *adj*

5) (In your classes) (at school), success (in mathematics) requires an <u>intuitive</u>

     n   *pp*   *art*   *n*   *pp*   *n*

sense (of the <u>rightness</u>) (of things).

      pro   *art*   *n*   *pp*   *art*   *n*   *art*   *adj*   *n*

6) You often give the solution (to the problem) an "educated" guess.

          pro   *art*   *n*   *pp*   *adj*   *n*   *pp*   *art*   *adj*   *n*

7) Sometimes you find the answer (without conscious awareness) (of the creative process).

      pp   *adj*   *n*   *pro*   *art*   *n*   *pp* *art*   *n*

8) (In your mind,) you instinctively know the answer (to the problem).

         n   *pp* *adj*   *n*   *pp*   *n*

9) Creativity exists (in all aspects) (of math).

     art *adj*   *n* *pp* *adj*   *n*   *art* *adj*   *adj*   *n* *pp* *n*

10) The <u>logical</u> part (of your mind) is not the only intellectual tool (in use).

Directions

Write what job the underlined words are doing in the sentence. Choose your answer from the following jobs:

             modifier   **object of the preposition**

Sentence #	Word	Job
2	mathematicians	*object of the preposition*
3	one's	*modifier*
5	intuitive	*modifier*
5	rightness	*object of the preposition*
10	logical	*modifier*

Application & Enrichment

Reading for Context

How many words do you think there are in the English language? Would you be surprised to learn that it's over 170,000?* There are an additional almost 50,000 *archaic* words that we don't use anymore. And each native English speaker only uses about 20,000–30,000 words on a regular basis. The more you read, the more words you will come across that you don't know! In a lot of cases, carefully reading the sentence and passage that the unfamiliar word is in can give you **context** clues to the word's meaning; you can get a pretty good idea of the meaning without having to look it up.

For example, we used the word *archaic* in the third sentence above: "There are an additional almost 50,000 *archaic* words that we don't use anymore." Read the sentence again, carefully. What do you think *archaic* means?

_____ Now, look up the definition or ask your instructor.

old, unused

Note: If an exact meaning is important, don't guess! Get out your dictionary or look up the meaning online!

The following sentences each contain an archaic English word in a modern English sentence. Reading for context, write your guess for what the word means. Then look up the meaning of the word and write the definition in the second blank. See how close you can get to the real meaning, but don't look it up until you've guessed!

Answers will vary.

1) I shouldn't have eaten the food from the street vendor because now I am *liverish*.
liverish
your guess: _____ meaning: _____
slightly ill, upset stomach

2) The dog *groked* at me unblinkingly the entire time I was eating my hamburger, silently begging with his eyes.
groked
your guess: _____ meaning: _____
to stare intently at someone who is eating,
in hopes that they will share with you

3) The old woman's *grimalkin* daintily licked its paws, cleaned its face, and curled up in front of the fireplace for an afternoon nap.
grimalkin
your guess: _____ meaning: _____
cat (esp. an old or gray one)

4) Since it was too dark to see, I *grubbled* under the car seat for my phone as best I could.
grubbled
your guess: _____ meaning: _____
to grope or feel for something you can't see

5) Honestly, I wasn't happy with anything hanging in my closet; I can't be expected to show up on the first day of school with only these *habiliments* to choose from!
habiliments
your guess: _____ meaning: _____
clothing, clothes

6) Because we did not want to be followed, we *jargogled* the directions so they were useless.
   jargogled
   your guess: _____   meaning: _____
   to confuse or mix up

7) Juan works very hard during the week, but on Saturdays, he is *otiose* to the point of not getting dressed, not showering, and not washing dishes all day.
   otiose
   your guess: _____   meaning: _____
   lazy or slothful

8) The big truck sped through the slushy puddle, *besmirching* my brand new white jacket with a splash of muddy snow.
   besmirch
   your guess: _____   meaning: _____
   to make dirty or discolored

9) After listening to the children *brabble* for an hour about whose turn it was to sit by the window, Mom threatened to turn the car around.
   brabble
   your guess: _____   meaning: _____
   to loudly argue, especially about unimportant things

10) The oxen pulling the *wain* could barely move it, because it was so loaded down with heavy sacks of grain.
   wain
   your guess: _____   meaning: _____
   wagon or cart

*2nd Ed Oxford English Dictionary 2020

Prepositional Phrases: Assessment

Directions

Mark all of the nouns (**n**), proper nouns (**pn**), adjectives (**adj**), articles (**art**), pronouns (**pro**), and prepositions (**pp**). Be sure to use wings, if necessary. On a separate sheet of paper, diagram the prepositional phrases. Remember that you can look at the notes pages if you need help.

Each correctly identified word or prepositional phrase is worth one point.

               n   *adj*   *n*   *pp*   *n*   *pp*   *adj*   *n*

$\frac{\quad}{10}$ **1)**   Men have no advantage (over women) (in mathematical <u>ability</u>).

        art   *n*   *pp*   *n* *pp* *art* *adj*   *n*   *pp* *adj*   *n*

$\frac{\quad}{18}$ **2)**   The perception (of math) (as a masculine domain) stems (from other myths)

       pp   *art*   *n*

       (about the <u>subject</u>).

           n   *pp*   *n*   *pp* *art*   *n*   *pp* *adj*   *adj*   *n*

$\frac{\quad}{13}$ **3)**   Ability (in math) is seen (as the triumph) (of <u>cool</u>, impersonal logic).

       pro   *pp* *art* *adj*   *adj*   *n* *pp* *n*

$\frac{\quad}{10}$ **4)**   This fits (with an outdated, stereotypical image) (of <u>men</u>).

       pp *adj*   *n*   *n*   *pp*   *n*   *pp*   *n*

$\frac{\quad}{11}$ **5)**   (In <u>some</u> cases,) students will not readily admit (to difficulty) (with math).

        pro   *pp* *adj*   *n*   *pp*   *adj*   *n*

$\frac{\quad}{16}$ **6)**   Others, early (in their schooling), begin believing (in personal <u>inadequacy</u>)

       pp *art* *n*   *pp*   *n*

       (as a reason) (for failure).

       pro *pp* *adj*   *n*   ——*pp*——   *n*   *art* *adj*   *n*

$\frac{\quad}{14}$ **7)**   All (of <u>these</u> students), (regardless of gender,) may be expressing the same fears

       pp   *n*

       (about math.).

            pp   *n*   *art*   *n*   *pp*   *n*   *pp* *art* *n*

__ **8)** (Throughout history), a variety (of people) have contributed (to the <u>field</u>)
15

        pp   *n*

(of mathematics).

        adj   *adj*   *n*   *pp* *adj* *n*   *pp*   *n*

__ **9)** Women's historical contributions (in this area) are being recognized (at last)
19

        pp   *adj*   *n*   *pp* *adj*   *adj*   *n*

(in award-winning films) and (in popular <u>nonfiction</u> books).

        adj   *n*   *pro*   *n*   *pp*   *n*   *

__ **10)** <u>Educated</u> people no longer believe that math comes more easily (for men) than
10

        pp   *n*

(for women).

Students may recognize than *as a possible preposition. In this sentence, it is actually acting as a subordinating conjunction, which is covered in Level 4. The prepositional phrase is* for women.

=====
136

Fill in the blank

____ **11)** The noun or pronoun at the end of the prepositional phrase is called the _____.
1   *object of the preposition*

____ **12)** Pronouns are words that _____.
1   *take the place of one or more nouns*

____ **13)** A proper noun begins with a _____.
1   *capital letter*

____ **14)** A common noun ☐ can ☒ cannot consist of more than one word.
1

=====
4

Directions

Write what job the underlined words are doing in the sentences. Choose your answer between the following:

modifier   **_object of the preposition_**

Five points each.

Sentence #	Word	Job
1	ability	_object of the preposition_
2	subject	_object of the preposition_
3	cool	_modifier_
4	men	_object of the preposition_
5	some	_modifier_
6	inadequacy	_object of the preposition_
7	these	_modifier_
8	field	_object of the preposition_
9	nonfiction	_modifier_
10	Educated	_modifier_

_50_

Diagrams

Enter score from diagramming solutions here.

_83_

Total Points $\dfrac{218}{273} = 80\%$

_273_

Lesson 4
Subject & Verb

Instructor Notes

It is important that students continue verbalizing so that you can be sure that they are understanding the jobs that the different parts of speech are performing in sentences. Work through the first few sentences with them until you are confident that they understand the new concepts.

For this lesson, we are adding Step 5 to the list of steps. Students will say, "_____ is a verb. Who or what _____?" They should answer the question and continue with, "_____ is the subject and _____ is the verb." The students should immediately draw a baseline (illustrated in the Student Notes) and write in the subject and verb. It's important to emphasize that neither the subject nor the verb will be inside a prepositional phrase.

This is also where the list of steps takes shape as "The Process." The Process is a systematic method, as you may have already seen with the steps, that will eventually allow students to identify every part of speech and its job in the sentence. It is a logical way of sorting the words for diagramming. While diagramming is a visual tool that students will eventually outgrow as they internalize grammar rules, they may find themselves unconsciously running through the steps of The Process whenever they write for the rest of their lives. Establishing the automaticity of choosing the proper parts of speech and using them correctly in their writing and speech is the ultimate goal of The Process and the program. This skill will be a lifelong benefit to students' ability to communicate effectively.

A Tip for Instructors

If a lesson seems overwhelming, slow the pace a bit and have your student split up each exercise by doing the odd-numbered sentences one day and even-numbered the next. This will give your student two weeks to complete the lesson instead of one.

Lesson 4: Subject & Verb

In English, there are two kinds of main verbs: action verbs and linking verbs. This lesson covers action verbs. We'll talk about linking verbs in Lesson 8.

First, here are some important definitions:

Action verb

Like its name suggests, an action verb expresses physical or mental action.

Example 1:   (physical action)   jump, carry, search, run, examine

(mental action)   worry, think, believe, consider

Subject

A verb has a subject. The subject is the noun or pronoun that is doing the action of the verb. To find the subject of a verb, you ask, "Who or what (say the verb)?"

art   n   pp   art   n   av   pp   art   adj   n
Example 2:   The horse (in the lead) raced (across the finish line).

The verb, or action, is **raced**. Who or what **raced**? The **horse raced**. So **horse** is the subject of **raced**.

Tip: Neither the subject nor the verb will ever be inside a prepositional phrase!

Some sentences will have words that look like a verb but don't have a subject. These are called **verbals**. We'll learn all about verbals in Level 4, but for now, just mark them with a **v**. If it does have a subject, then it's a real verb, and for now, mark it **av**.

pn   av   —v—   art pn pp adj   n
Example 3:   Joe hopes to get an A (on this test).

"To get" looks like a verb, but if you ask, "Who or what *to get*?", there is no answer in the sentence. A subject and verb always work together. "Joe hopes" sounds right because the noun and verb work together. That's because "Joe" is a third person singular noun and "hopes" is a third person singular verb. But "Joe to get" just doesn't work together, does it?

Tip: Many verbals end in *-ing*, and any verb with *to* in front of it (like *to get* in our example above) is always a verbal—more about verbals in later lessons.

Here are a few more useful definitions:

Sentence

A sentence expresses a complete thought. It must *always* have a subject and a verb, or it's not a sentence. A sentence can be either a statement or a question (exclamations and commands are just different types of statements).

art   adj   adj   n   av   pp   art   n
Example 4:   The sleek, black dog barked (at the moon).

Simple subject

The simple subject is the noun or pronoun that is doing the action of the verb, without any modifiers. In Example 4 above, **_dog_** is the simple subject of the sentence.

Predicate

In a sentence, a predicate is everything that is not the subject. So in our example about the sleek, black dog, the predicate is **_barked at the moon_**.

Simple predicate

The simple predicate is just the verb by itself, without any modifiers. In the example above, **_barked_** is the simple predicate. (We'll learn about verb modifiers in the next lesson.)

Diagramming

You have already started doing a little diagramming with the prepositional phrases in the previous lesson. Now we're going to learn how to diagram complete sentences! For the rest of the lessons that include diagramming, we will call going through the steps and diagramming the sentence "The Process." Don't worry, we will start slowly, and you're already familiar with the steps to take to get started. We will be adding a new step to help you identify the verb. Each of the answers to the questions asked in the steps has its own place in a sentence diagram.

I) How to Diagram the Subject and Verb

A diagram shows the structure of a sentence by making a picture of it. Every diagram starts with a **baseline** which holds the subject and verb. A baseline looks like this:

This is what it looks like when you add a short sentence to it:

Example I: *n*   *av*
             Lions roar.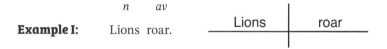

Notice that the baseline is a horizontal line and that the subject and verb are separated by a short vertical line that crosses the horizontal line.

In a sentence diagram, capitalize the first word of the sentence, but don't include punctuation.

II) How to Find the Subject and Verb

First, parse the sentence by following all of the steps you have been using to find nouns (**_n_**), articles (**_art_**), adjectives (**_adj_**), pronouns (**_pro_**) and prepositions (**_pp_**), putting parentheses around prepositional phrases.

Second, mark any word that looks like a verb with a **_v_**. For each **_v_**, ask, "Who or what (say the verb)?" The answer, a noun or pronoun, will be the subject of that verb. For this lesson, when you find the subject, mark its verb with **_av_** for **_action verb_**. (Remember that some words that look like verbs will be verbals and will not have subjects. Just leave those words marked with **_v_**.)

Now that you have identified the subject and verb, write the simple subject and simple predicate (remember, that's the verb) on the baseline.

Example II: Before diagramming anything, parse the sentence.

adj   n   av adj   n   adj   n

My uncle runs five miles every morning.

- The verb is **runs**.

- Ask, "Who or what runs?" Answer: **uncle**. Because **runs** has a subject, you can mark it with **av**. (If there were more verbs without subjects, you would just leave them marked **v**.)

- The simple subject is **uncle**. The simple predicate is **runs**. Write these on your baseline.

III) How to Diagram Articles and Adjectives

Articles and adjectives are diagrammed on diagonal lines attached under the noun or pronoun they modify. They should be diagrammed in the order in which they appear in the sentence.

adj adj   n   av

Example III: Our special guest sang.

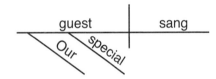

IV) How to Diagram a Prepositional Phrase

If a prepositional phrase modifies a noun, it will answer the question "which?" just like the other modifiers (articles and adjectives) you've learned. In this lesson, if a prepositional phrase modifies the subject, you will diagram it. In the first example sentence we used in this lesson, **The horse in the lead raced across the finish line**, the prepositional phrase **in the lead** tells you which horse. Here's how you will diagram that:

Example IV:
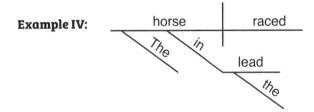

For now, don't worry about diagramming prepositional phrases that are modifying words other than the subject.

V) How to Diagram a Command

Diagramming a command or request might appear tricky because it seems there is no subject.

Example V: Brush your teeth.

The verb is **brush**, but if you ask "Who or what brush?" the sentence doesn't say! For commands or requests, the subject is an understood "you." That means that, without saying it, it's clear that the sentence is talking about "you." The diagram will look like this:

(you)	Brush

Notice that **you** is in parentheses. That shows that it is "understood." That means that we know to whom the command is addressed. Also notice that **Brush** is capitalized; that shows that it is the first word in the sentence.

VI) How to Diagram an "Inverted" Sentence

Inverted sentences are sentences that begin with **here** or **there**.

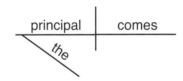

Example VI: Here comes the principal.

We use these sentences all the time in English, but they could be confusing to diagram. Once you find the verb **comes** and ask "Who or what *comes*?", it's clear that the subject is **principal**. It can seem confusing, because you're used to seeing the subject in front of the verb. That's why we call these sentences "inverted," which means "turned upside down."

The chart on the next page, which we call "The Process," shows the mental steps you must go through to analyze a sentence's grammar. We will be adding steps to this chart, but for now, it only includes the ones you already know.

The Process

Step 1. Find and mark *n* over all the nouns in the sentence (*pn* over proper nouns, with wings, if needed).

Step 2. Find all the articles (*art*) and adjectives (*adj*)—ask, "Which (noun)?" Remember to use wings over all of the words of a proper adjective, if needed.

Step 3. Find all the pronouns (*pro*).

Step 4. Find all the prepositions (*pp*) and put parentheses ( ) around the prepositional phrases.

Step 5. Find all words that look like verbs and mark them *v*.

Step 6. For each **v**, ask "Who or what (verb)?"

No answer?
It's a verbal.
Leave it marked **v**
and move on.

Answer? It's an action verb.* Mark it with **av**. The answer to your question is the simple subject. The action verb is the simple predicate. Draw a baseline and fill in the simple subject and the simple predicate.

Complete your diagram with the modifiers that go with the simple subject (don't forget prepositional phrases).

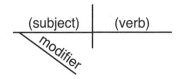

*The next few lessons focus on action verbs only, so you can mark all verbs you find that have subjects as **av**. In Lesson 8, you will learn about another kind of verb.

Subject and Verb: Exercise A

Directions

Steps 1–4. Parse the sentences by marking all of the nouns (***n***), proper nouns (***pn***), adjectives (***adj***), articles (***art***), pronouns (***pro***), and prepositions (***pp***). Put parentheses around each prepositional phrase.

Step 5. Find all words that look like verbs and mark them with ***v***.

Step 6. Ask, "Who or what (verb)?" If there is an answer, mark the verb as an action verb (***av***) and fill in the baseline of your diagram with the simple subject (the answer to the question) and simple predicate (the action verb).

Diagram the subject, its modifiers, and the action verb, using a separate sheet of paper, if necessary. You don't need to diagram anything else at this point.

1)   <u>People</u> (from <u>Mexico</u>) settled (in Texas) starting (in the seventeenth century).
   n *pp* *pn* *av* *pp* *pn* *v* *pp* *art* *adj* *n*

2)   These people came (to Texas) (before the settlement) (by the Europeans).
   adj *n* *av* *pp* *pn* *pp* *art* *n* *pp* *art* *pn*

3)   They established farms and ranches (in the territory).
   pro *av* *n* *n* *pp* *art* *n*

4)   <u>These</u> early settlers plowed the land.
   adj *adj* *n* *av* *art* *n*

5)   Their crops grew (in the harsh Texan climate).
   adj *n* *av* *pp* *art* *adj* *adj* *n*

6)   These Texans gave Spanish names (to their <u>towns</u>).
   adj *pn* *av* *adj* *n* *pp* *adj* *n*

7)   They called one (of these towns) San Antonio.
   pro *av* *pro* *pp* *adj* *n* ——*pn*——

        adj   *n*   *av*   *pp*   *pn*   *pp*   *art*   *adj*   ——*pn*——

8) Mexican culture spread (from Texas) (throughout the <u>southwestern</u> United States).

         av   *adj* *adj* *adj*   *n*

9) There went these early Texas pioneers.

(See Lesson Notes, Section VI)

  art   *n* *pp* *adj* *n*   *av*   *pp* *art*   *n* *pp* *adj*   *adj*   *n*

10) The names (of these states) <u>resulted</u> (from the influence) (of these Spanish-speaking settlers).

(See Lesson Notes, Section IV)

Fill in the blank

11) A verb cannot be an action verb unless it has a _____.
     subject

12) The articles in English are _____, _____, and _____.
     a, an, the

Directions

Write what job the underlined words are doing in each sentence. Choose your answers from the following:

    subject   ***object of the preposition***   ***verb***   ***modifier***

Sentence #	Word	Job
1	People	*subject*
1	Mexico	*object of the preposition*
4	These	*modifier*
6	towns	*object of the preposition*
8	southwestern	*modifier*
10	resulted	*verb*

Subject and Verb: Exercise B

Directions

Complete Steps 1–4 of The Process. Next, identify all of the words that look like verbs and mark them with **v**. Then ask, "Who or what (verb)?" until you find the subject and action verb. Mark the action verb with **av**. The action verb is the simple predicate. Finally, diagram the simple subject and its modifiers and the simple predicate. You don't need to diagram anything else yet.

```
            —————pn————        av  art   n    pp   art  adj    adj       n    pp   pn
```
1) Roberto Felix Salazar wrote a poem (about the early Mexican settlers) (of Texas).

```
        adj      n     av   art   n     v    pp   pn
```
2) These people settled the land known (as Texas).

```
      adj         adj         n    av   ——v——  art  n   pp  art      n      pp  adj
```
3) This Mexican-American poet wanted to tell the story (of the contributions) (of these

```
        adj      n
```
Texas pioneers).

```
      adj   adj     adj      n    av    adj      adj        n            n
```
4) This joyful, passionate poem describes these hard-working farmers and ranchers.

```
       pro   av   adj     adj       adj     n    pp   art  adj  adj    n
```
5) They built their thick-walled adobe houses (from the dry Texas earth).

```
       adj     adj      n    av          ——v——  adj      n
```
6) Devout Catholic people struggled mightily to build their churches.

```
       adj      adj       n     av    ——v——   n   pp  adj      n
```
7) Strong Mexican pioneers sacrificed to make homes (for their families).

```
       av   adj   n   pp  adj   adj       n
```
8) Read this poem (at your first opportunity).

(See Lesson Notes, Section V)

```
       adj   adj    adj      n    av  art adj    n
```
9) These brave Mexican settlers left a rich legacy.

art adj   adj   n   pp adj   n   av   pp adj   n

10) The soft Spanish names (of their <u>towns</u>) survive (to this day).

Fill in the blank

11) If there are any words between a preposition and its object, they are _____.

   modifiers

12) _____ can consist of more than one word.

   Proper nouns   Proper adjectives is another possible answer.

13) If a word looks like a verb but doesn't have a subject, it's a _____.

   verbal

Directions

Write what job the underlined word is doing in each sentence. Choose your answers from the following:

   subject   **object of the preposition**   **verb**   **modifier**

Sentence #	Word	Job
1	Roberto Felix Salazar	*subject*
3	poet	*subject*
4	describes	*verb*
5	adobe	*modifier*
6	struggled	*verb*
7	families	*object of the preposition*
8	Read	*verb*
10	towns	*object of the preposition*

Subject & Verb: Exercise C

Directions

Complete Steps 1–4 of The Process. Next, identify all of the words that look like verbs and mark them with ***v***. Then ask, "Who or what (verb)?" until you find the subject and action verb. Mark the action verb with ***av***. The action verb is the simple predicate. Finally, diagram the simple subject and its modifiers and the simple predicate. You don't need to try to diagram anything else yet.

      pro *av* *art*   *n*   *pp*   *adj*   *n*   *pp* *adj* *n* *pp*   *n*

1) Today we study the contributions (to American culture) (from all <u>sorts</u>) (of people).

     ——————*pn*————— *av* *adj*   *n* *pp* *adj*   *n*

2) Roberto Felix Salazar <u>took</u> obvious pride (in his ancestors).

     ——————*pn*————— *pp* —————*pn*————— *av*   *art*   *n*

3) "The Other Pioneers" (by Roberto Felix Salazar) celebrates the accomplishments

  pp *adj*   *adj*   *n*

(of <u>these</u> Texas pioneers).

       pn   *pp* *art*   *adj*   ——*pn*——   *av*   *pp* *adj*   *adj*   *n*

4) Mexican-Americans (in the southwestern United States) identify (with these rugged <u>people</u>).

      n   *pp* *adj*   *n*   *av*   *adj*   *n*   *pp* *art* *adj*   *n*

5) Settlers (from all nations) left their mark (on the <u>Texas</u> landscape).

     adj   *n*   *av* ——*v*—— *pp*   *pro* *pp* *art*   *adj*   *n*   *pp* *adj*   *n*

6) American students try to learn (about all) (of the different contributions) (to our culture).

     pp *art* *n*   *av*   *art* *n* *pp* *adj*   *adj*   *n*

7) Here (on the land) remain the marks (of these early settlers).

(See Lesson Notes, Section VI)

     adj   *n*   *av*   *art* *n* *pp* *art*   *adj*   *pn*

8) Mexican-American culture really <u>shapes</u> the life (of the American Southwest).

      n   *pp* *adj* *pro* *av* *pro* ———*v*——— *pro* *pp* *adj*   *n*

9) Poems (like this one) help us to understand more (about our country).

            av   *adj*   *n*   *n*   *pp* *adj*   *n*

10) Please read these stories and poems (about our <u>ancestors</u>).

Fill in the blank

11) In a diagram, a _____ goes on a diagonal line attached to another word.

     modifier

12) Pronouns are words that _____.

     take the place of nouns

13) Adjectives are words that _____.

     modify (or describe) nouns and pronouns

Directions

Write what job the underlined word is doing in the sentence. Choose your answers from among the following:

    subject   ***object of the preposition***   ***verb***   ***modifier***

Sentence #	Word	Job
1	sorts	*object of the preposition*
2	took	*verb*
3	these	*modifier*
4	people	*object of the preposition*
5	Texas	*modifier*
8	shapes	*verb*
10	ancestors	*object of the preposition*

Application & Enrichment

Comma Splices

The reason we study grammar and punctuation is to learn how to communicate our ideas in ways that our readers can easily understand. Punctuation provides guidance to those readers so that they know when a thought is complete, what information is essential to the idea, and even what your attitude is about what you are writing.

Level 5 of *Analytical Grammar* focuses on many different punctuation and word usage rules, but now that you can define a sentence, you can be aware of a very common, confusing punctuation error that can detract from understanding. It's called a **comma splice**.

Commas are the "yield" signs of punctuation. When used correctly, they tell your reader to mentally pause in the flow of the text. When used incorrectly, however, they can cause your reader to stumble and interfere with clear communication.

To splice is to join two things together so that they become one thing. For example, two ropes can be spliced together by weaving the strands of one rope with the strands of the other so that the two parts become one rope.

A **comma splice** is when you use only a comma to join two sentences. Comma splices are sometimes called **run-on sentences**, and it's easy to see why. Look at this example:

> We spent the whole day at the beach, we had the sunburn to prove it!

We spent the whole day at the beach and *we had the sunburn to prove it* are both independent clauses. They are complete sentences on their own, so we have two sentences that run together ("run on") with no clear stopping and starting point. When you write a sentence with a comma splice, your reader is faced with jumbled-together ideas that have a pause rather than a full stop between the end of one thought and the beginning of the next.

There are several ways we could fix this problem.

- Just write two separate sentences:
  We spent the whole day at the beach. We had the sunburn to prove it!

- Join the sentences with a conjunction, such as *and,* after the comma:
  We spent the whole day at the beach, and we had the sunburn to prove it!

- Join the sentences with a subordinating conjunction, such as *since* (Level 4):
  Since we spent the whole day at the beach, we had the sunburn to prove it!

- Join the two sentences with a semicolon (Level 5):
  We spent the whole day at the beach; we had the sunburn to prove it!

While you won't learn about numbers 3 and 4 until later lessons, you can start using numbers 1 and 2 right now!

Directions

The following sentences include a comma splice. Fix the comma splice by rewriting each sentence in two ways: First, write it as two sentences, using a capital letter at the beginning and a period at the end of each sentence. Next, include a conjunction after the comma. Choose from **and, but,** or **or** for this exercise, since we haven't studied conjunctions yet.

Possible solutions are provided; your student may choose a different conjunction or punctuation mark.

1) The bees are busy with the flowers in the garden, they are happily buzzing around.

The bees are busy with the flowers in the garden. They are happily buzzing around.
The bees are busy with the flowers in the garden, and they are happily buzzing around.

2) I hope the baseball game is played today, it's raining really hard right now.

I hope the baseball game is played today. It's raining really hard right now.
I hope the baseball game is played today, but it's raining really hard right now.

3) My cat got out of the house yesterday, she was as frightened as I was!

My cat got out of the house yesterday. She was as frightened as I was!
My cat got out of the house yesterday, and she was as frightened as I was!

4) We might go to the pool today, we might go to the movies if it rains.

We might go to the pool today. We might go to the movies if it rains.
We might go to the pool today, or we might go to the movies if it rains.

5) I will loan you my favorite book, I want to make sure you read it.

I will loan you my favorite book. I want to make sure you read it.
I will loan you my favorite book, and I want to make sure you read it.

Subject & Verb: Assessment

Directions

Mark all the nouns, proper nouns, articles, adjectives, pronouns, prepositions, action verbs, and verbals in the following sentences. Put parentheses around the prepositional phrases. Then, on a separate sheet of paper, diagram the simple subject and simple predicate of each sentence. Add the modifiers for the subject to your diagram, including any articles, adjectives, and prepositional phrases.

Remember to use your notes if you need help.

Each correctly identified word or prepositional phrase is worth one point.

$\frac{}{9}$ **1)**
    av adj adj   n   pp   adj adj   n
Study this beautiful poem (about Texas's early settlers).

$\frac{}{13}$ **2)**
  n   pp   adj   n   av   art   n   pp adj adj n
Students (of American culture) read the literature (of all our poets).

$\frac{}{8}$ **3)**
  pro av   n   pp   adj   adj   n
They want information (about America's early settlers).

$\frac{}{14}$ **4)**
  n   pp adj n   av   n   pp adj n pp   n
Students (in this school) read examples (of this type) (of literature).

$\frac{}{8}$ **5)**
  pro av adj   n   pp adj   n
They want more information (about their roots).

$\frac{}{10}$ **6)**
  art   n   pp adj n av pro ———v——— pro
An understanding (of our roots) helps us to understand ourselves.

$\frac{}{13}$ **7)**
  adj   adj   pn   av art adj   n pp adj
Many inquisitive Americans appreciate the numerous contributions (of America's

  adj   adj   n
different cultural groups).

$\overline{17}$ **8)**
art   adj   n   pp   pn   av   art   adj   n   pp   n   pp   adj   n

The best writers (in America) created a great body (of work) (on this subject).

$\overline{13}$ **9)**
adj   n   pp   adj   adj   n   av   pro   n   pp   pro

Great literature (about our early ancestors) gives us pride (in ourselves).

$\overline{8}$ **10)**
av   adj   adj   n   pp   adj   n

Here comes that positive self-esteem (from our ancestors)!

$\overline{\overline{113}}$

Fill in the blank

____ **11)** A verb is a "real" verb when it has a _____.

1   subject

____ **12)** The articles in English are _____, _____, and _____.

3   a, an, the

____ **13)** Which kind of noun begins with a capital letter? _____

1   a proper noun

____ **14)** Which kind of noun consists of only one word? _____

1   a common noun

____ **15)** A pronoun is a word that _____.

1   takes the place of one or more nouns

____ **16)** Adjectives are words that _____.

1   modify nouns and pronouns

____ **17)** If a word looks like a verb but doesn't have a subject, it's a _____.

1   verbal

$\overline{\overline{9}}$

Directions

Write what job the underlined words are doing in the sentences. Choose your answers from among the following:

| subject | object of the preposition | verb | modifier |

Five points each

Sentence #	Word	Job
1	Study	verb
2	American	modifier
3	settlers	object of the preposition
4	Students	subject
5	more	modifier
6	understanding	subject
7	groups	object of the preposition
8	work	object of the preposition
9	gives	verb
10	self-esteem	subject

50

Diagrams

Enter score from diagramming solutions here.

34

Total Points $\dfrac{165}{206} = 80\%$

206

Lesson 5
Adverbs

Instructor Notes

Your student should continue verbalizing as this new part of speech is added to the steps of the Process. When identifying adverbs modifying verbs, students should be able to say that a certain adverb tells you *how* or *when* or *where* or *why* about the verb.

An important point that can't be overemphasized is that **adverbs or prepositional phrases that are modifying a verb can almost always be moved** to other parts of the sentence without changing the meaning at all or sounding awkward. This is a key trick to knowing that a verb is being modified. If, however, moving the adverb or prepositional phrase changes the meaning or makes the sentence sound awkward, that is a sign that it is modifying a different part of speech and must stay next to that word.

For example, in the sentence "Today we are learning about adverbs," the adverb *today* can be moved to several different places without changing the meaning of the sentence at all. That tells us that it modifies the verb *are learning*. In the sentence "We are working very hard," the adverb *very* can't be moved away from the word *hard* without losing the meaning of the sentence. This means that it is modifying *hard*.

Review the three "tests" described in the Student Notes. Does the modifier (adverb or prepositional phrase) answer *how* or *when* or *where* or *why* about the verb? Can it be moved around? If neither of those tests give a definite answer, try the "read it together" test.

A note on scoring

As students gain confidence with their grammar identification skills, you may find yourself in a debate about which word is being modified, especially by prepositional phrases. If your student knows enough to argue their case for the placement of a modifier, even if it differs from what's given in the solution, go ahead and give them credit for it. That means that they need to be able to give a logical reason based on what they have learned, such as, *"You can move it to multiple places in the sentence without changing the meaning,"* or, *"It tells us **when** about the verb,"* rather than, *"It's next to the noun,"* or, *"It just looks right."* Some points of grammar are open to interpretation and are debated among the most qualified experts in the field without a resolution. It is exciting to see students gain enough confidence with grammar to be able to argue for their opinion.

Lesson 5: Adverbs

An **adverb** is a versatile **modifier** that can modify a **verb**, an **adjective**, or another **adverb**.

Let's discuss the parts of speech an adverb can modify.

1) When an adverb modifies a **verb**, it tells you in **one word** "how?", "when?", "where?", or "why?" about that verb.

art   *n*   *av*   *adv*   *adv*

Example 1:   The students arrived promptly today.

What does *promptly* tell you? It tells you **how** the students *arrived*. It is an adverb, so it is marked **adv.**

What does *today* tell you? It tells you **when** the students *arrived.* It is also an adverb and is also marked **adv.**

Here's how we diagram adverbs. It should look familiar, except that rather than modifying a noun like our other modifiers do, these modifiers are modifying a verb.

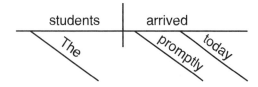

Adverbs that modify verbs can be moved!

This is extremely important and that's why we're going to make such a big deal about it! This fact will be extremely helpful to you when it comes to figuring out what an adverb modifies. Words in English usually have to be in a certain place in a sentence (for example, articles must come before nouns, subjects usually come before verbs, and prepositions usually come at the beginning of a prepositional phrase) but that's not true of **adverbs that modify verbs**. You can almost always move such adverbs to two or three different places in the sentence without it sounding odd or changing the meaning in any way. Let's try it with the sentence in Example 1, above. Can *promptly* be moved around? How about *today*?

    a) Today the students arrived promptly.

    b) The students promptly arrived today.

    c) The students arrived today promptly.

All of these variations make complete sense, don't they? There are probably a few more that we aren't listing here, too. So if you find a word in a sentence that can be moved without changing the sentence's meaning, that tells you two things about that word:

    a) It's an adverb, and

    b) It modifies the verb!

If there's an adverb that **can't** be moved away from another word without changing the meaning of the sentence, that means that it is modifying that word and needs to stay where it is. That brings us to the other two parts of speech that an adverb can modify.

2) Adverbs that modify **adjectives** tell you "how?" or "to what extent?" about the adjective.

art   adv   adj   n   av pp art   adj   n

Example 2: The extremely nervous patient sat (in the dentist's chair).

What does *extremely* tell you? It tells you **how** nervous. *Nervous* is an adjective describing the patient, and *extremely* is an adverb modifying *nervous* by telling you HOW nervous the patient was. Try moving *extremely* to other places in the sentence. It changes the meaning, doesn't it? In fact, it doesn't even make sense anywhere else in the sentence. That's how we know that it is an adverb modifying an adjective, not a verb. Placed anywhere else in the sentence, it changes the meaning, and it doesn't even make sense!

Here's how you will diagram an adverb modifying an adjective.

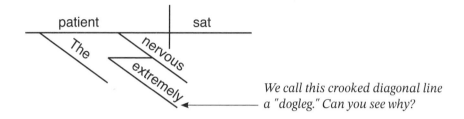

We call this crooked diagonal line a "dogleg." Can you see why?

Remember those prepositions that aren't prepositions that we mentioned in Lesson 3?

Now you're ready to know more about them, because you know what an adverb is!

art   n   av   pp?   pp   art   n

Example: The man drove away (from the house).

Away sure looks like a preposition, doesn't it? It often is. But it's not in a prepositional phrase in this sentence (it doesn't have an object), so it can't be a preposition. It's an **adverb**, because it's telling us *where the man drove.* There is a prepositional phrase: ***from the house.*** It also answers the question, "Where did the man drive?" In this case, we do have a preposition (*from*), because it has an object of the preposition (*house*).

So remember: if you see a stray word that looks like a preposition but doesn't have an object, it's probably an adverb!

3) Adverbs that modify other adverbs tell you "how?" or "to what extent?" about that adverb.

adj   n   av   adv   adv

Example 3:   Our guest left quite abruptly.

First, what does ***abruptly*** tell you? It tells you how your guest ***left***. *Abruptly* is an adverb that modifies the verb *left*. Our guest didn't take their time saying their goodbyes—they *left abruptly*. What does *quite* tell you in this sentence? It tells you ***how abruptly*** our guest left. It wasn't just abruptly, it was ***quite*** abruptly! *Quite* is an adverb because it is modifying another adverb, *abruptly*. Try to move it away from the word *abruptly*. It doesn't make sense anywhere else in the sentence. That is your way to double-check.

Diagramming an adverb that is modifying an adverb also uses a dogleg, this time attached to the adverb it is modifying.

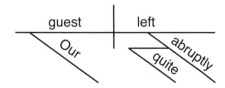

> Use a dogleg every time you have a modifier that modifies another modifier.

In fact …

Prepositional phrases can modify verbs and other modifiers, too! You can use the same questions to test them: "how?", "when?", etc. If they answer the question, they are acting like an adverb, and you will use a dogleg to diagram them. Here's how that looks:

pro av   n   pp   art   n

Example 4A: We ate lunch (in the park).

(*in the park* tells you where we *ate*)

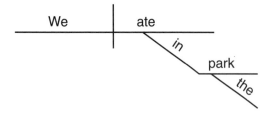

We know that *in the park* must modify the verb *ate* because we can move it to other places in the sentence and the meaning doesn't change. *In the park we ate lunch* still tells us the same thing.

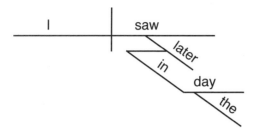

Example 4B: I saw him later (in the day).

pro av pro adv pp art n

(*in the day* tells you "later when?" or "later to what extent?")

In the day can't be moved away from its position following *later* without changing the meaning of the sentence or making it nonsense. So we know that, since it can't be moved away, this prepositional phrase is modifying *later*.

A few more notes

- Many adverbs end in *-ly*. In English, you can change many adjectives (for example, *beautiful*) into adverbs by adding the suffix *-ly* (*beautifully*). Not all adverbs end in *-ly*, however, and not all words that end in *-ly* are adverbs. Only adjectives with the added *-ly* suffix are adverbs.

- The words *how, when, where,* and *why* are often adverbs, so mark them that way for now while parsing and diagramming sentences.

- If you really can't figure out what a word is, there's a good chance that it's an adverb!

Here's one more check you can do to determine what's being modified:

When you're having a hard time figuring out where a modifier (adverb or prepositional phrase) goes, try saying the modifier together with the word you think it modifies. For instance, in Example 4b, *saw in the day* doesn't sound right, but *later in the day* does! This tells you that *in the day* goes with *later*. Add this to the movability trick and using the questions (*how, when, where,* or *why*), and these three methods will almost always show you what an adverb or a prepositional phrase is modifying.

Adverbs: Exercise A

Directions

Mark all of the nouns (**n**), proper nouns (**pn**), adjectives (**adj**), articles (**art**), pronouns (**pro**), and prepositions (**pp**) in the paragraph below. Put parentheses around the prepositional phrases. Identify all of the words that look like verbs and mark them with **v**. Then ask, "Who or what (verb)?" until you find the subject and action verb. Mark the action verb with **av**. The action verb is the simple predicate. Mark all adverbs with **adv**. Use your notes if you need help. The first one is done for you.

| | pro | av | ——————pn—————— | pp art adv adj adj | pn |

Example: We recognize Dr. Martin Luther King, Jr. (as a truly great Black American).

——pn—— adv av art adj adj n

1) Dr. King certainly had a brilliant, well-disciplined mind.

pp art adv adj n pn adv av n

2) (At a very young age), King sadly experienced prejudice.

art adj n adv av adv pp art adj n

3) The White children always played separately (from the Black children).

pro av adj pn adv

4) This bothered young Martin deeply.

pro adv av pp art adj n pp adj n

5) He always wondered (about the unequal treatment) (of his people).

pp n pn adv av pp ——————pn—————— pp pn

6) (At fifteen,) King proudly enrolled (at Morehouse College) (in Atlanta).

——pn—— av adv pp adj n pp n

7) Dr. King worked diligently (for his future) (in life).

pro adv av art n pp adj n

8) He finally chose the ministry (as his profession).

adj ——pn—— adv av adj n pp adj adj n pp n

9) Young Dr. King always inspired his congregation (with his fiery sermons) (against injustice).

Fill in the blank

10) A pronoun is a word that _____.

takes the place of one or more nouns

11) An antecedent is _____.

the noun that the pronoun stands for

12) Adverbs are words that modify _____, _____, and _____.

verbs, adjectives, other adverbs

13) If an adverb can be moved within a sentence, it modifies a _____.

verb

14) If an adverb cannot be moved, it modifies _____.

an adjective or adverb (or the word it must stay next to)

Directions

Write what job the underlined word is doing in the sentence. Choose your answers from the following:

subject   **object of the preposition**   **verb**   **modifier**

Sentence #	Word	Job
Example	American	*object of the preposition*
1	certainly	*modifier*
2	age	*object of the preposition*
3	always	*modifier*
4	This	*subject*
5	treatment	*object of the preposition*
6	enrolled	*verb*
8	finally	*modifier*
9	fiery	*modifier*

Adverbs: Exercise B

Directions

Complete Steps 1–6 of The Process. Then mark all adverbs with **adv.**

Be on the lookout—there is a sneaky preposition made up of two words in today's sentences! Look back at the notes for Lesson 3 if you need help finding it.

On a separate sheet of paper, diagram the simple subject, simple predicate, and all of their modifiers (adjectives, adverbs, and prepositional phrases). You don't need to diagram anything else at this point.

Diagramming solutions are found at the end of this book.

—————pn—————   adv   av   pp   ————pn————

1) <u>Martin Luther King, Jr.</u> ultimately graduated (from Morehouse College).

pro   adv   av   art   n   pp ————————pn————————

2) He then <u>received</u> a scholarship (to Crozer Theological Seminary).

art   n   pp ————pn————   adv   av   —pn—

3) The teachings (of Mahatma Gandhi) <u>totally</u> fascinated Dr. King.

pp   adj   n   pn   adv   av   adj   n   pp   adj   n

4) (With nonviolent <u>methods</u>), Gandhi successfully freed his people (from British domination).

pn   adv   av   pp   art   n   pp   adj   n

5) King sincerely believed (in the <u>success</u>) (of this method).

pro   av   adv   pp   adj   adj   n   pp   ————pn————

6) <u>He</u> studied hard (for his doctoral degree) (at Boston University).

pp   adj   n   ——pn——   av   adj   adj   n   pp   art   adv   adj   n

7) (Upon his graduation), Dr. King started his adult life (as the very young <u>pastor</u>)

pp art   n   pp   pn

(of a church) (in Alabama).

pp   adj   n   pp   adj   n   art   n   av   art   n   pp   art   n

8) (At that time) (in our <u>history</u>), the law mandated the separation (of the races).

```
     pp adj    adj      n      —pn—   adv    av    adj  adj    n
```
9) (In his Sunday sermons,) Dr. King <u>bravely</u> denounced these unjust laws.

```
     —pp—    —adj—   n    art  adj    n    pp  art     n     adv   av    art
```
10) (Because of Dr. King's words), the <u>Black</u> leaders (in the community) also favored the

```
     n   pp    adj      n
```
use (of Gandhi's methods).

Short answer

11) Which kind of noun begins with a lowercase letter and consists of only one word?

a common noun

12) If a word looks like a verb but it doesn't have a subject, what is it called?

a verbal

13) If you find a verb and ask, "Who or what (say the verb)?", what are you looking for?

the subject

Directions

Write which job the underlined words are doing in each sentence. Choose your answers from the following:

subject *object of the preposition* *verb* *modifier*

Sentence #	Word	Job
1	Martin Luther King, Jr.	*subject*
2	received	*verb*
3	totally	*modifier*
4	methods	*object of the preposition*
5	success	*object of the preposition*
6	He	*subject*
7	pastor	*object of the preposition*
8	history	*object of the preposition*
9	bravely	*modifier*
10	Black	*modifier*

Adverbs: Exercise C

Directions

Complete Steps 1–6 of The Process. Then mark all adverbs with **adv.**

On a separate sheet of paper, diagram the simple subject, simple predicate, and all of their modifiers (adjectives, adverbs, and prepositional phrases). You don't need to diagram anything else at this point. *Diagramming solutions are found at the end of this book.*

   ——adj——   n   pp   adj   n   pp   adj   n   adv   av   art

1) Dr. King's <u>message</u> (about non-violent resistance) (to segregation laws) certainly struck a

   n   pp   art   n   pp   adj   pn

chord (in the hearts) (of many Americans).

   ————pn————   pp   art   adj   n   pp   n   av   art   n   pp   art

2) <u>Mrs. Rosa Parks,</u> (with a simple act) (of bravery), provided an opportunity (for the

   n   pp   ——adj——   n   pp   n

implementation) (of Dr. King's plan) (of action).

   pp   art   n   pp   adj   n   ——pn——   adv   av   pp   art   ——adj——   n   pp   art

3) (Against the laws) (of her city), Mrs. Parks simply sat (in a "Whites Only" <u>section</u>) (of a

   adj   n

city bus).

   art   adj   n   adv   av   pro   pp   adj   n

4) The city police <u>quickly</u> arrested her (for her "crime.")

   ——pn——   adv   av   art   adj   n   pp   adj   n   pp   art   adj   n

5) Dr. King promptly <u>organized</u> the Black citizens (of that city) (in a bus boycott).

   art   ————pn————   adv   av   art   adj   n   pp   n

6) The Selma Bus Company soon <u>suffered</u> the daily loss (of money).

   adv   ——pn——   av   adj   n   pp   n   pp   adj   adv   adj   n

7) Now Dr. King <u>led</u> non-violent marches (in protest) (against these completely unjust laws).

```
          adv    pp ————pn———— art ————————pn———————— av  art   n    pp
```

8) Finally, (on <u>November 12, 1956</u>), the United States Supreme Court issued a decision (in

```
          n     pp   adj   adv   adj        n
```

support) (of these civil rights crusaders).

```
          pp ————————pn———— pp  pn  ——pn——  av  art adv   adj      adv  adj
```

9) (In Washington, D.C.,) (in 1963), Dr. King delivered a very beautiful and <u>now</u> historic

```
          n    pp  adj  n   pp  adj    n    pp   pn
```

speech (about his dream) (of racial equality) (for America).

```
          adv    pp  pn art adj    n     av  art  n  pp adj  adv  adj    adj    n
```

10) Tragically, (in 1968,) a White <u>ex-convict</u> ended the life (of this truly great American hero).

Fill in the blank

11) The three articles are _____.

a, an, and the

12) A proper noun begins with a _____ and may consist

of _____.

capital letter, more than one word

13) An action verb expresses _____ and must have a _____.

mental or physical action, subject

14) If a word looks like a verb but doesn't have a subject, it's a _____.

verbal

Directions

What jobs are the underlined words doing in the sentences? Choose your answers from among the following:

subject   *object of the preposition*   *verb*   *modifier*

Sentence #	Word	Job
1	message	*subject*
2	Mrs. Rosa Parks	*subject*
3	section	*object of the preposition*
4	quickly	*modifier*
5	organized	*verb*
6	suffered	*verb*
7	led	*verb*
8	November 12, 1956	*object of the preposition*
9	now	*modifier*
10	ex-convict	*subject*

Application & Enrichment

Synonyms Activity 1

As we've already discussed, there are over 170,000 words in the modern English language, but we only use about 20,000-30,000. Many common words have **synonyms**, or other words that mean (almost!) the same thing. We say *almost* because there are often very subtle differences between the synonyms, particularly with verbs, adjectives, and adverbs. Having the ability to replace a general word with a specific synonym that says exactly what you mean adds spice and interest to your writing. For example, read the following sentences:

Mom is *mad* at us for playing the same song fifty times in a row.

We get it: Mom is not pleased with us. Now look at the following sentences with synonyms in place of *mad*. Rank them in order of how *mad* Mom is, with 1 being "eh, she's not that mad," up to 5 being "oops, we went too far—beware the wrath of Mom!"

_____1_____ Mom is *annoyed* with us for playing the same song fifty times in a row.

_____5_____ Mom is *furious* with us for playing the same song fifty times in a row.

_____3_____ Mom is *irritated* with us for playing the same song fifty times in a row.

_____4_____ Mom is *livid* with us for playing the same song fifty times in a row.

_____2_____ Mom is *exasperated* with us for playing the same song fifty times in a row.

You can probably make an argument for a slightly different order than the one we provided in the solutions, but nonetheless, a *furious* Mom is more angry than an *annoyed* Mom. The sentences subtly change in meaning based on our word choice. That's why it's a good idea to practice the skill of finding synonyms for commonly used words in our writing.

Directions

Using a thesaurus, dictionary, or online resource, find three good quality synonyms for the following words. What we mean by "good quality" is words that you could actually use in your writing. For fun, find one outlandish synonym, too: one you would probably never use, but that's just a fun—or funny!—word!

Answers will vary. Some possible suggestions are listed.

	quality synonym 1	quality synonym 2	quality synonym 3	just for fun!
big	*immense*	*gigantic*	*substantial*	*commodious*
said	*asserted*	*suggested*	*replied*	*opined*
good	*satisfactory*	*superb*	*favorable*	*stupendous*
sad	*heartbroken*	*wistful*	*mournful*	*woebegone*
happy	*cheerful*	*contented*	*elated*	*chipper*
very	*absolutely*	*exceedingly*	*particularly*	*prodigiously*
nice	*friendly*	*kind*	*delightful*	*ducky*
many	*countless*	*frequent*	*several*	*multitudinous*
interesting	*thought-provoking*	*intriguing*	*fascinating*	*engrossing*
walked	*hiked*	*raced*	*strolled*	*perambulated*

Bonus word: This is a word we tend to use a lot today to describe things that are really good or exciting. Can you come up with three quality synonyms (not *good* or *exciting*) and one just for fun?

awesome	*impressive*	*mind-blowing*	*awe-inspiring*	*stupefying*

Adverbs: Assessment

Directions

Complete Steps 1–6 of The Process. Then mark all adverbs with **_adv_**.

On a separate sheet of paper, diagram the simple subject, simple predicate, and all of their modifiers (adjectives, adverbs, and prepositional phrases). You don't need to diagram anything else at this point.

Remember to look at your notes if you need any help; also remember that adverbs modifying the verb can be anywhere in the sentence!

Each correctly identified word or prepositional phrase is worth one point.

       art   n   pp art ————pn————   adv   av   ————————pn————————

__ **1)** The crowds (at the Lincoln Memorial) joyfully received Martin Luther King, Jr.
9

      adj   pn   av   adj   n pp adj   adv   adj   n

__ **2)** All Americans take tremendous pride (in this beautifully eloquent speech).
11

      adj   pn   pp adj   n   adv   av   pro pp art n

__ **3)** Many Americans (in that generation) instantly hailed him (as a hero).
13

      adv adj   n   av   pn   pp adj   n

__ **4)** Today, his courage inspires Americans (of all colors).
9

      ————pn————   av   n   pp art adv   adj   n   pp art   n

__ **5)** Dr. King emphasized discipline (as a very important aspect) (of the struggles)
16

      pp   n

(against injustice).

      ————pn————   av   pn   pp art   n   pp   n   pp adj   n

__ **6)** Dr. King reminded Americans (of the guarantee) (of equality) (for all people)
18

      pp adj   pn

(in our Constitution).

      adv   art ————pn————   av adj   n pp art   n pp adj   n

__ **7)** Constitutionally, the Founding Fathers formed this country (as a home) (for all people).
14

          n   pp   adj   n   pp art   n   av   pp adj adj   n   pp   n

___ **8)** <u>People</u> (from all corners) (of the world) come (to this sweet land) (of liberty).
18

          adv   ———pn———   av   pn   pp art   n pp adj adv   adj   n

___ **9)** Tragically, James Earl Ray <u>robbed</u> America (of the life) (of this truly great man).
14

          adv   pn   pp adj   n   av   art   n   pp adj   n   pp   n

___ **10)** Today, Americans (of all <u>colors</u>) remember the courage (of this man) (of peace).
16

‗‗
138

Fill in the blank

___ **11)** A noun is the name of _____.
1   *a person, place, thing, or idea*

___ **12)** A _____ noun begins with a lowercase letter.
1   *common*

___ **13)** A _____ noun begins with a capital letter.
1   *proper*

___ **14)** A _____ noun can consist of only one word.
1   *common*

___ **15)** An adjective is a word that _____.
1   *modifies a noun or a pronoun*

___ **16)** The articles in English are _____, _____, and _____.
3   *a, an, the*

___ **17)** A pronoun is a word that _____.
1   *takes the place of a noun*

___ **18)** An antecedent is _____.
1   *the noun the pronoun stands for*

___**19)** A word may look like a preposition, but it's not unless it has a(n) _____.

1   *object*

___**20)** Adverbs modify _____, _____, and _____.

3   *verbs, adjectives, adverbs*

14

Directions

Write what job the underlined words are doing in the sentences. Choose your answers from among the following:

    subject   ***object of the preposition***   ***verb***   ***modifier***

Five points each

Sentence #	Word	Job
1	crowds	*subject*
2	speech	*object of the preposition*
3	hailed	*verb*
4	Today	*modifier*
5	aspect	*object of the preposition*
6	Dr. King	*subject*
7	home	*object of the preposition*
8	People	*subject*
9	robbed	*verb*
10	colors	*object of the preposition*

50

Diagrams

Enter score from diagramming solutions here.

$$\overline{\overline{}}$$
48

$$\underline{\overline{}} \; \textit{Total Points} \quad \frac{200}{250} = 80\%$$
250

Lesson 6
Sentence Patterns 1 & 2

Instructor Notes

This lesson introduces the first two of the five basic sentence patterns. Pattern 1 will be familiar to students because it only has a subject and an action verb on the diagram's baseline. These sentences are diagrammed in the same way as they learned in Lesson 5.

Pattern 2 adds the identification of a direct object. One problem that may occur is that, when asking "(subject) (verb) what?" (the question they will be able to answer if there is a direct object), they may try to find an answer even when there isn't one. Emphasize to them that the answer to this question tells you **what**, not when or where or how. When students ask "(subject) (verb) what?", it's just as likely that there will be NO answer as it is that there WILL be one!

In this lesson, students are introduced to the concept of "stripping down" the sentence, which means removing **all** modifiers—articles, adjectives, adverbs, and prepositional phrases—regardless of what they are modifying. Whatever is left will go on the baseline. If one noun or pronoun is left over, the sentence is Pattern 1. If two nouns and/or pronouns are left over, then the sentence is Pattern 2.

The Process Chart is updated to include this question.

A Tip for Instructors

Consider asking your student to diagram half of the sentences in an exercise; if they understand the concept and can identify the word, phrase, or clause that is the focus of the lesson, they may not need to diagram every sentence.

Lesson 6: Sentence Patterns 1 & 2

Now that you know the basics of diagramming, the next step is to learn about the **five basic sentence patterns.** No matter how different sentences may look, no matter how complicated or how simple they seem, they all fall into one of five patterns. We have already learned about **action verbs**. The first three sentence patterns contain **action verbs only**.

To make it easier to identify sentence patterns, first remove all of the modifiers: articles, adjectives, adverbs, and prepositional phrases. Strip the sentence down to just nouns and verbs.

Pattern 1: N-V

A diagram of the N-V pattern only has two items on the baseline: a subject (**N**) and an action verb (**V**). The presence of these two parts of speech is the minimum requirement for a sentence: it must have a subject and a verb. You have already been diagramming some of these sentences, beginning in Lesson 4! The simple subject and simple predicate may have modifiers, and there may be prepositional phrases, but **there will be no other nouns or verbs**.

	art	n	av	pp	art	adj	n
Example 1:	The	boy	stood	(on	the	boat's	deck).

As you have already learned, this sentence should be diagrammed like this:

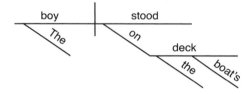

Pattern 2: N-V-N

For this pattern, we need to introduce a new job that nouns can do. It's called a **direct object**. If the subject is a noun that is *doing* the verb's action, the direct object is the noun that has the verb's action *done to it*. The direct object is receiving the action of the verb. If a sentence is Pattern 2, after you remove all the modifiers you will be left with two nouns and a verb. All of these parts of speech may have their own modifiers, but there will be no other nouns or verbs in the sentence.

To figure out which noun is the direct object:

- First find the subject and verb.

- Say "(subject)(verb) what?"

The answer will be a noun or pronoun that is called the **direct object**.

	adj	adj	n	av	art	adj	n
Example 2:	My	best	friend	had	a	birthday	party.

When we remove all the modifiers, we are left with *friend*, *had*, and *party*. Start with the verb to find the subject. **Who or what** *had*? *Friend had*. So *friend* is the subject. *Friend had* **what**? *Friend had* **party**. *Party* is the direct object.

The diagram for this Pattern 2 sentence looks like this:

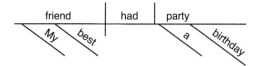

Notice that the vertical line between subject and predicate extends below the baseline, while the vertical line between the verb and the direct object does not.

The Process

Now we can add another step to The Process that we introduced in Lesson 4. Step 7 is asking "(subject) (verb) what?" to determine if there is a direct object. Here's the updated flowchart for this lesson.

Step 1. Find and mark *n* all the nouns in the sentence (*pn* for proper nouns).

Step 2. Find and mark all articles (*art*) and adjectives (*adj*) by asking, "which (noun)?"

Step 3. Find and mark all the pronouns (*pro*).

Step 4. Find and mark all the prepositions (*pp*). Put parentheses around all prepositional phrases.

Step 5. Find and mark any word that looks like a verb (*v*).

Step 6. Ask, "Who or what (verb)?"

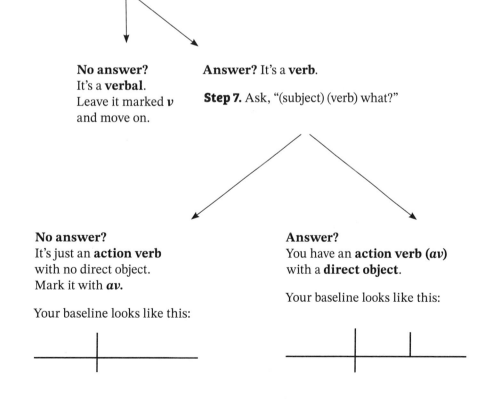

No answer?
It's a **verbal**.
Leave it marked *v*
and move on.

Answer? It's a **verb**.

Step 7. Ask, "(subject) (verb) what?"

No answer?
It's just an **action verb**
with no direct object.
Mark it with *av*.

Your baseline looks like this:

Answer?
You have an **action verb (*av*)**
with a **direct object**.

Your baseline looks like this:

Sentence Pattern 1: Exercise A

Directions

All of the sentences in this exercise are Pattern 1. Parse them and put parentheses around the prepositional phrases. Then diagram the subject, verb, and all of their modifiers. You know how to diagram every part of speech in these sentences—be proud of all that you have learned so far! Remember that you can use your notes if you need help.

Diagramming solutions are found at the end of this book.

    adj   adj   n   av pp adj   n
1) Many Americans' <u>grandparents</u> live (in other states).

     pro   pp pro av pp adj   adj   n   adv   adv
2) Many (of us) <u>go</u> (to our grandparents' houses) very rarely.

     n   pp   adj   n   adv   av pp adj   n   pp   art   n   pp
3) People (in former generations) seldom moved (to other <u>places</u>) (with the frequency) (of

     adj   n
today's families).

     adj   adj   n   av pp art adj   n   pp   adj   n
4) Most American children <u>lived</u> (in the same town) (as their grandparents).

     pro   av   adv   pp adj   adj   n
5) They visited often (in <u>their</u> grandparents' homes).

     pp   adj   adj   adj   n   pro   av   pp   art   n   pp adj   n
6) (During these long, frequent visits) they learned (about the lives) (of their <u>grandparents</u>).

     n   pp   pn   adv av pp adj   n   pp   adj   n
7) Children (in America) today <u>visit</u> (with their grandparents) (during short vacations).

     n   pp   adj   adj   n   av   adv   pp   n   pp   n
8) Families (from all economic <u>levels</u>) move frequently (from place) (to place).

     art adj pro av   pp adj   n   pp art adj   n
9) A lucky <u>few</u> visit (with their grandparents) (for a long time).

       pp   art   n   pp   adv   adj   n   av pp pro pp adj   n

10)   (Before the <u>end</u>) (of your grandparents' lives), speak (to them) (of your gratitude)

       pp adj adj   n

      (for all their love.)

      (See Lesson 4 Notes, Section V.)

Fill in the blank

11) Pronouns are words that _____.

     take the place of nouns

12) To find the direct object, you say the _____ , say the _____ , and ask _____ .

     subject, verb, what

13) A word that looks like a verb but doesn't have a subject is a _____ .

     verbal

Directions

Write what job the underlined words are doing in the sentences. Choose your answers from among the following:

subject   *object of the preposition*   *verb*   *modifier*

Sentence #	Word	Job
1	grandparents	*subject*
2	go	*verb*
3	places	*object of the preposition*
4	lived	*verb*
5	their	*modifier*
6	grandparents	*object of the preposition*
7	visit	*verb*
8	levels	*object of the preposition*
9	few	*subject*
10	end	*object of the preposition*

Sentence Pattern 2: Exercise B

Directions

All of the sentences below are Pattern 2, so all of them have direct objects. Parse the sentences and put parentheses around the prepositional phrases.

Now diagram the entire sentence. Remember to use The Process Chart in the notes and follow the steps to find the subject, verb, and direct object. Strip down the sentence by removing all of the modifiers (articles, adjectives, adverbs, and prepositional phrases). Use the proper baseline shown in Step 7. We've given you some help on the first one.

Diagramming solutions are found at the end of this book.

    pp   *adj*   *adj*   *n*   *pro* *adv*   *av*   *art*   *n* *pp* *adj*   *n*

1) (In today's youth-oriented society) we seldom appreciate the <u>wisdom</u> (of our elders).

What is the verb? _____

    appreciate

Ask, "Who or what (verb)?" _____

    The answer to this question is the subject.   *we*   *appreciate*

Ask, "(subject) (verb) what?" "_____ what?" _____

    The answer to this question is the direct object.   *we*   *appreciate*   *wisdom*

    art   *n*   *av*   *adj*   *adj*   *n*   *pp* *adj*   *adj*   *n*

2) The <u>past</u> gives many valuable lessons (for our modern lives).

    adj   *n*   *adv*   *adv*   *av*   *adj*   *n*   *pp* *art*   *n* *pp* *art* *n*

3) Young people today rarely show their <u>appreciation</u> (for the lessons) (of the past).

    adj   *n*   *adv*   *av*   *n*   *pp*   *adj*   *n*

4) <u>Older</u> people sometimes lack patience (with younger people).

    adj   *n*   *adv*   *av*   *n*   *pp*   *n*

5) These conflicts occasionally cause <u>misunderstandings</u> (between generations).

    art   *adj*   *n* *pp* *art* *adj*   *n*   *av*   *n*   *pp* *art* *n* *pp* *pro*

6) An enjoyable hour (with an older <u>person</u>) opens doors (from the past) (for you).

       adj   *n*   *pp*   *art* *n*   *av*   *n*   *pp*   *n*   *pp* *adj* *adv*   *adj*   *n*

7) These doors (from the past) shed <u>light</u> (on things) (in our often confusing world).

       adj   *adj*   *n*   *pp*   *adj*   *n*   *adv*   *av* *n*   *pp*   *adj*   *n*

8) Some older people (in <u>nursing</u> homes) never get visits (from younger people).

      art *n* *pp* *pro*   *av*   *pro* *pp* *pro*

9) A visit (like this) benefits <u>both</u> (of you)!

      av   *n*   *--pp--* *adj* *adj*   *n*   *pp* *art*   *n*   *pp* *art* *adj*   *n*

10) <u>Take</u> time (out of your busy life) (for a visit) (with an older person).

    (See Lesson 4 Notes, Section V.)

Directions

Write what job the underlined words are doing in each sentence. Choose your answers from the following:

subject	object of the preposition	verb
modifier	direct object	

Sentence #	Word	Job
1	wisdom	*direct object*
2	past	*subject*
3	appreciation	*direct object*
4	Older	*modifier*
5	misunderstanding	*direct object*
6	person	*object of the preposition*
7	light	*direct object*
8	nursing	*modifier*
9	both	*direct object*
10	Take	*verb*

Sentence Patterns 1 & 2: Exercise C

Directions:

The sentences below are either Pattern 1 or Pattern 2. Parse the sentences and put parentheses around the prepositional phrases.

Use The Process Chart in the notes and follow the steps to find the subject, verb, and whether there is a direct object. Strip down the sentence by removing all of the modifiers (articles, adjectives, adverbs, and prepositional phrases). Then choose the correct baseline for either Pattern 1 or Pattern 2. Diagram the entire sentence.

    ————pn———— *av   art   n   pp   adj   n*

1) Rudolfo A. Anaya wrote a <u>story</u> (about his grandfather).

    adj adj   n   av pp art   n   pp art ——pn—— *pp* ——pn——

2) This old <u>farmer</u> lived (in a valley) (on the Pecos River) (in New Mexico).

    adj   n   av   n   pp   n

3) Anaya's culture teaches respect (for <u>elders</u>).

    pro av pp adj   adj   n   pp   art   n

4) He lived (on his <u>grandfather's</u> farm) (during the summer).

    adj   n   adv   av pp adj   n   pp   art   adj   n

5) His uncles <u>also</u> lived (in that valley) (beside the grandfather's farm).

    adj   n   av adj n   pp   n

6) Anaya's grandfather used few words (for <u>advice</u>).

    av   pp   n

7) "<u>Pray</u> (for rain)."

    pp   adj   n   pp art   n   adj   pn   av pp   n pp   n

8) (Beside his grandfather) (in the wagon), young Rudolfo <u>drove</u> (into town) (for supplies).

art   adj   n   pp adj   n   av   pp art adj   adj   n

9) The beloved <u>grandfather</u> (of his childhood) died (after a long, useful life).

pn   av   art adj   n   pp   n   pp   adj   adj   n   pp   adj   n

10) Anaya gained a great <u>deal</u> (of wisdom) (from his close association) (with his grandfather).

Directions

Write what job the underlined words are doing in each sentence. Choose your answers from among the following:

subject	object of the preposition	verb
modifier	direct object	

Sentence #	Word	Job
1	story	direct object
2	farmer	subject
3	elders	object of the preposition
4	grandfather's	modifier
5	also	modifier
6	advice	object of the preposition
7	Pray	verb
8	drove	verb
9	grandfather	subject
10	deal	direct object

Application & Enrichment

Synonyms Activity 2

Synonyms add spice and interest to our writing. Using specific, descriptive words instead of general words helps to create a mental picture for the reader that shows exactly what we are describing. Here is a sentence with some pretty generic words:

The vehicle drove on the roadway.

Come up with three more specific words for each of the following words. We've given you an example to help you get thinking. Be creative!

Answers will vary. Some possible answers have been provided.

vehicle	bicycle	sports car	cement truck	tractor
drove	wobbled	raced	lumbered	chugged
roadway	trail	highway	street	pathway

Now, plug your specific words into the sentence:

along

Example: The <u>bicycle</u> <u>wobbled</u> <s>*on*</s> the <u>trail</u>.

Notice that we changed the preposition *on* to *along* because *along the trail* communicates what we want to say better than *on the trail*, in our opinion. Don't just plug in your words without looking at how they work in the entire sentence! If you want to change an existing word, just cross it out and write your new word above.

Answers will vary.

1) The _____ _____ on the _____.
          (vehicle)   (drove)   (roadway)

2) The _____ _____ on the _____.
          (vehicle)   (drove)   (roadway)

3) The _____ _____ on the _____.
          (vehicle)   (drove)   (roadway)

Look at your new sentences and compare them to the original. Do they paint a more vivid mental picture for a reader? Ask your instructor for their opinion.

Keep these words handy, because we will use them for the Application & Enrichment activity in Lesson 7!

Sentence Patterns 1 & 2: Assessment

Directions

Parse the sentences below and put parentheses around the prepositional phrases. Then, on a separate sheet of paper, diagram the entire sentence. Remember to use The Process. You can look at your notes if you need help.

Each correctly identified word or prepositional phrase is worth one point.

art adj n   av   adv   pp art n   pp art n

— 13 **1)** An old man sat quietly (on a <u>bench</u>) (in the park).

adj   n   pp art   n   av art n   pp   n   pp art adj   adj   n

— 18 **2)** <u>Some</u> boys (from the neighborhood) played a game (of baseball) (in a nearby vacant lot).

pn av art n   pp art   n   pp art adj adj   n

— 14 **3)** Paul hit the <u>ball</u> (over the fence) (onto the old man's bench).

art   n   pp adj   n   av pp   adj   n

— 11 **4)** "The baseball (from our game) <u>fell</u> (onto your bench)."

adj   n   adv av pro pp art   n

— 9 **5)** "Your baseball nearly hit <u>me</u> (on the head)!"

pp art adj   n   pn   av   pp art adj n

— 12 **6)** (In a polite tone), Paul <u>apologized</u> (to the old man).

pro   adv   av adv adj   n

— 6 **7)** "You certainly have <u>very</u> nice manners."

pro av   n   pp art n

— 7 **8)** "I played baseball (as a <u>boy</u>)."

art adj adj n   pp art   n   av   art   n

— 11 **9)** The kind old <u>man</u> (on the bench) returned the baseball.

$$\begin{array}{c} \text{art} \quad \text{adj} \qquad n \qquad\qquad pp \qquad \text{art} \quad \text{pro} \quad \text{av} \quad pp \quad \text{adj} \quad \text{adj} \qquad n \qquad pp \quad \text{art} \quad n \end{array}$$

$\frac{}{17}$ **10)** A real friendship (between the two) grew (from this chance <u>encounter</u>) (in the park).

$\frac{\overline{\overline{}}}{118}$

Directions

Write what job the underlined words are doing in each sentence. Choose your answers from among the following:

subject	***object of the preposition***	***verb***
modifier	***direct object***	

Five points each

Sentence #	Word	Job
1	bench	*object of the preposition*
2	Some	*modifier*
3	ball	*direct object*
4	fell	*verb*
5	me	*direct object*
6	apologized	*verb*
7	very	*modifier*
8	boy	*object of the preposition*
9	man	*subject*
10	encounter	*object of the preposition*

$\frac{\overline{\overline{}}}{50}$

Diagrams

Enter score from diagramming solutions here.

$$\frac{}{68}$$

$$\frac{}{236} \; \textit{Total Points} \quad \frac{189}{236} = 80\%$$

Sentence Pattern 3

Instructor Notes

This is another lesson that students often find easy, as long as they are stripping the sentence of all modifiers before they try to determine the sentence pattern. Once all articles, adjectives, adverbs, and prepositional phrases have been removed, if there are three nouns and/or pronouns left, then it's Pattern 3. And the middle one is *always* the indirect object!

Lesson 7: Sentence Pattern 3

Sentence Pattern 3: N-V-N-N

This pattern introduces a new job that nouns can do: the **indirect object**. An indirect object is the noun or pronoun *for whom* or *to whom* an action is performed.

Start by parsing the sentence, then strip it down, removing all of the modifiers, Sentence Pattern 3 consists of four main parts in this order: the **subject (N)**, an **action verb (V)**, an **indirect object (N)**, and a **direct object (N)**. All four of these parts may have modifiers, and there may be prepositional phrases in the sentence, but once these are removed, there are **no other nouns or verbs**.

After you strip down the sentence, count the number of nouns or pronouns left over. If you have one noun left over, you have a Pattern 1 (N-V) sentence. If you have two left over, it's a Pattern 2 (N-V-N) sentence. If you have three nouns left over, you have Pattern 3 (N-V-N-N): the first noun is the subject, the second is the indirect object, and the third is the direct object.

A sentence can't have an **indirect object** unless it has a **direct object**!

Look at this sentence to see what this looks like in action:

$$pn \quad av \quad pro \quad art \quad n \quad pp \quad n$$

Example 1:   Mom gave me a dollar (for candy).

If you strip down this sentence, what is left?

Mom   *gave*   *me*   *dollar*

What is the verb? ***gave***

Who is doing the action of the verb? ***Mom***

What did she give? ***dollar***

Whom did she give it TO? ***me***

Below is how you diagram a Pattern 3 sentence:

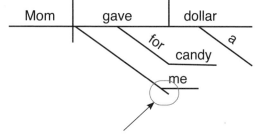

Notice the little "tail."

It looks very similar to the way we diagram prepositional phrases, but notice that it has a little tail. Do you remember that we called the way we diagram prepositional phrases a "dogleg"? Well, we call the way we diagram an indirect object a "broken dogleg" because of the little tail!

Important Note!

The **indirect object** will **ALWAYS** be located **between** the verb and the direct object in the sentence. The words will **always** come in this order:

subject – verb – indirect object – direct object

Pattern 3 sentences will only contain **action verbs**.

If you have three nouns left after you strip the sentence down, the middle one is always the indirect object.

Sentence Pattern 3: Exercise A

Directions

All of these sentences are Pattern 3 sentences. Parse them and put prepositional phrases in parentheses. Strip each sentence of all of the modifiers (articles, adjectives, adverbs, and prepositional phrases) to find the N-V-N-N pattern. Beneath each sentence, write the subject (*n*), action verb (*av*), indirect object (*n*), and direct object (*n*) in order. Use your notes if you need help. The first one has been done for you.

	adj	pn	av	pn	adj	adj	n	pp	pn

Example: Black Americans gave America many great <u>members</u> (of Congress).

Americans – gave – America – members

1) ——pn—— av pn adj adj n pp adj n pp pn

<u>Blanche Kelso Bruce</u> gave Missouri its first school (for Black students) (in 1864).

Blanche Kelso Bruce – gave – Missouri – school

2) pp pn art adj n av ——pn—— art n pp art n

(In 1874,) the Mississippi legislature gave <u>Mr. Bruce</u> the honor (of the role)

pp art adj adj adj n

(of the state's first Black senator).

legislature – gave – Mr. Bruce – honor

3) pp pn ——pn—— av ——pn—— adj adj adj n pp pn

(In 1888), Henry Plummer Cheatham gave North Carolina its first Black member (of <u>Congress</u>).

Henry Plummer Cheatham – gave – North Carolina – member

4) pp adj n pp pn pn av ——pn—— art n pp adv

(After his defeat) (in 1892), Cheatham built North Carolina an <u>orphanage</u> (for two

adj n

hundred children).

Cheatham – built – North Carolina – orphanage

5) ——pn—— pp ——pn—— av ——pn—— adj

Wood High School (in Charleston, South Carolina), provided <u>Robert Carlos DeLarge</u> his

adj n

early education.

Wood High School – provided – Robert Carlos DeLarge – education

6)   pp   pn   art ——adj——   n   av   pro   art   n   pp   adj   n
    (In 1870,) the South Carolina legislature <u>assigned</u> him the responsibility (of land commissioner)

pp   n   pp   adv   adj   adj   n
(in charge) (of that state's public lands).

legislature – assigned – him – responsibility

7)   adj   n   pp   adj   n   av   pro   art   n   pp art n pp   n   pp art
    His success (in that role) provided <u>him</u> a nomination (to the role) (of representative) (of the

——————————*pn*——————————
Second Congressional District).

success – provided – him – nomination

8)   pp   pn   pn   av   art ——pn—— adj adj adj   n   pp art adj   n
    (In 1966,) Massachusetts gave the United States its first <u>Black</u> senator (from a popular election).

Massachusetts – gave – United States – senator

9)   ——————————*pn*——————————   av   art   n   pp   pn   adj   n
    Senator Edward William Brooke III brought the people (of Massachusetts) twelve <u>years</u>

pp   adj   n   pp art   pn
(of dedicated service) (in the Senate).

Senator Edward William Brooke III – brought – people – years

Directions

Write what job the underlined words are doing in each sentence. Choose your answers from among the following:

subject **direct object** **indirect object**

object of the preposition **verb** **modifier**

Sentence #	Word	Job
Ex.	members	*direct object*
1	Blanche Kelso Bruce	*subject*
3	Mr. Bruce	*indirect object*
4	Congress	*object of the preposition*
5	orphanage	*direct object*
6	Robert Carlos DeLarge	*indirect object*
7	assigned	*verb*
8	him	*indirect object*
9	Black	*modifier*
10	years	*direct object*

Sentence Pattern 3: Exercise B

Directions

The sentences below are either Sentence Pattern 2 (N-V-N) or Pattern 3 (N-V-N-N). Parse the sentences and put the prepositional phrases in parentheses.

Then, on a separate piece of paper, diagram each sentence. Remember to strip each sentence of all modifiers (articles, adjectives, adverbs, and prepositional phrases) to find the sentence pattern. Use your notes if you need help.

1)
   adj   *pn*   *av*   *pn*   *pp* *adj*   *n*   *pp* *adj*   *n*
Black Americans represent America (in all aspects) (of our culture).

2)
   ———*pn*———   *av*   *art*   *adj*   ——*pn*——   *pro* *pp* *adj*   *adj*
Mary McLeod Bethune gave the southeastern United States one (of its finest

             adj   *n*
teacher-training institutions).

3)
   art   ——*pn*——   *av*   ——*pn*——   *art*   ———*adj*———   *n*   *pp*
The Brooklyn Dodgers gave Roy Campanella the "Most Valuable Player" award (in

   adj   *adj*   *n*
three different years).

4)
   ——*pn*——   *av*   *adv*   *adj*   *adj*   *n*   *pp*   *adj*   *n*
Wilt Chamberlain broke almost every scoring record (in professional basketball).

5)
   pp   *pn*   ——*pn*——   *av* *art*   *adj*   *n*   *pp*   *art*   *n*   *pp* *art* *adj*   *n*
(In 1839,) Joseph Cinque led a successful revolt (against the captain) (of a slave ship).

6)
   ——*pn*——   *av*   *adj*   *n*   *adj*   *n*   *pp*   *art*   *adj*   ———*pn*———
Harriet Tubman gave many slaves their freedom (through the famous Underground Railroad).

7)
   pp   *adj*   *adj*   *n*   *pp*   *n*   *pp*   *pn*   ———*pn*———   *av*
(After his own escape) (to freedom) (in 1835), Frederick Douglass denounced

   n   *pp* *adj*   *adj*   *n*
slavery (in his fiery speeches).

———*pn*———   *av*   *art*   ———————————————*pn**———————————————

8) W.E.B. Dubois <u>founded</u> the National Association for the Advancement of Colored People.

———*pn*———   *av*   *art*   *n*   *adj*   *adj*   *n*   *pp*   ————*pn*————

9) James Baldwin gave the <u>world</u> such magnificent essays (as "The Fire Next Time)."

———*pn*———   *av*   *art*   —————————*pn*—————————   *pp*   ———*pn***———

10) Lorraine Hansberry won the New York Drama Critics' Circle Award (for *A Raisin in the Sun*).

**The title of this organization includes two prepositional phrases that your student may mark.
However, because they are part of the title, they are not diagrammed separately as prepositional phrases.*

***Again, this title contains a prepositional phrase that your student may mark but that is not
diagrammed separately.*

Directions

Write what job the underlined words are doing in each sentence. Choose your answers from among
the following:

subject   **direct object**   **indirect object**

object of the preposition   **verb**   **modifier**

Sentence #	Word	Job
1	America	*direct object*
2	United States	*indirect object*
3	award	*direct object*
4	every	*modifier*
5	Joseph Cinque	*subject*
6	slaves	*indirect object*
7	slavery	*direct object*
8	founded	*verb*
9	world	*indirect object*
10	*A Raisin in the Sun*	*object of the preposition*

Sentence Pattern 3: Exercise C

Directions

The sentences in this exercise are either Pattern 1 (N-V), Pattern 2 (N-V-N), or Pattern 3 (N-V-N-N). Parse each sentence and put parentheses around the prepositional phrases.

Then, on a separate piece of paper, diagram each sentence. Remember to strip each sentence of all modifiers to find the sentence pattern. Use your notes if you need help. Diagramming solutions are found after the index.

      ————pn————   av   n   pp   adj   adj   n   pp   art   adj   n

1) Langston Hughes achieved <u>fame</u> (from his magnificent poems) (about the Black experience)

     pp   pn

(in America).

      ————pn————   av   adj   n   pp   art   n   pp   ————pn————

2) Langston Hughes <u>made</u> his entrance (into the world) (in Joplin, Missouri),

     pp   ————pn————

(on February 1, 1902).

     adj   n   av   art   n   pp   pn   pp   art   n   pp   n   pp   n

3) His father left the family (for Mexico) (in a fit) (of <u>rage</u>) (over discrimination).

     adj   n   av   adj   n   art   adj   n   pp   adj   n

4) His mother gave her <u>son</u> the best home (within her power).

     adv   n   pp   adj   n   av   pro   art   n   pp   adj   n

5) His classmates (in grammar school) gave him the <u>title</u> (of class poet).

     pp   adj   adj   n   pn   av   adj   n   pp   n   pp   pro

6) (On that same day,) Hughes wrote sixteen verses (in praise) (of them).

     pp   adj   adj   n   pn   av   pp   pn   pp   adj   adj   n   pp   adj   n

7) (At his father's request,) <u>Hughes</u> moved (to Mexico) (in his junior year) (of high school).

     pro   av   adj   adj   n   pp   adj   adj   n

8) He published his first <u>poem</u> (during his senior year).

       pn   *av*   *pro*   *pp*   ——*pn*——   *pp*   *pn*

9)   Hughes put himself (through Lincoln College) (in Pennsylvania).

           pp   *adj* *adj*   *n*   ——*pn*—— *av*   *pn*   *art* *adj*   *n*

10) (Throughout his long career,) Langston Hughes gave <u>America</u> the priceless <u>legacy</u>

    pp adj   *n*

(of his <u>poetry</u>).

Directions

Write what job the underlined words are doing in each sentence. Choose your answers from among the following:

subject	***direct object***	***indirect object***
object of the preposition	***verb***	***modifier***

Sentence #	Word	Job
1	fame	*direct object*
2	made	*verb*
3	rage	*object of the preposition*
4	son	*indirect object*
5	title	*direct object*
7	Hughes	*subject*
8	poem	*direct object*
10	America	*indirect object*
10	legacy	*direct object*
10	poetry	*object of the preposition*

Application & Enrichment

Synonyms Activity 3

In the last Application & Enrichment, we looked at how using different, specific words when we write creates a more vivid word picture for readers. There's an easy way to take our descriptive writing up yet another notch! That's where modifiers—adjectives and adverbs—come in: they tell more about our nouns and verbs, clarifying even more the picture we are painting with words.

Let's look back at our previous, improved example sentence:

The vehicle drove on the road.

became

The bicycle wobbled along the trail.

We get a clearer picture of what's happening with these new, more specific synonyms in place. But we can make it even better by adding some modifiers. We know that adjectives describe nouns, so we can brainstorm some adjectives to describe *bicycle* and *trail*. Adverbs do the same thing for verbs (and other parts of speech), so let's come up with some for those, too. Have fun—visualize the effect you want to paint with your words. In our sentence, we want to suggest that the bicycle is neither new nor stable:

bicycle (adjectives)	ancient	decrepit	rusty	rickety
wobbled (adverbs)	uneasily	alarmingly	precariously	hazardously
trail (adjectives)	rocky	wooded	rugged	muddy

Choose your favorite from the sentences you created for the last Application & Enrichment in Lesson 6. Visualize the scene you are trying to describe. Then brainstorm four words each to describe the synonyms you put in your sentence that replaced the following:

_____ (adjectives)   _____ _____ _____ _____

(vehicle)

_____ (adverbs)   _____ _____ _____ _____

(drove)

_____ (adjectives)   _____ _____ _____ _____

(road)

Now, plug these descriptors into your sentence. Here's our example sentence about the bicycle with the new modifiers we've chosen:

The ancient bicycle wobbled alarmingly along the rocky trail.

How much clearer and more vivid is that word picture? Remember that you can change the preposition if you need to, like we did! We also changed the order of the verb and adverb. It sounded better to us to say *wobbled alarmingly*, although *alarmingly wobbled* is also grammatically correct. You can do the same thing if you think it sounds better.

The _____ _____ _____ _____ on the _____ _____.
      (adj)   (vehicle)   (adv)   (drove)   (adj)   (road)

Sentence Pattern 3: Assessment

Directions

Parse the sentences below and put prepositional phrases in parentheses. Then, on a separate sheet of paper, diagram the sentences. Use your notes if you need any help.

Each correctly identified word or prepositional phrase is worth one point.

       adj   pn   av   art ——pn—— adj   n pp adj   n pp   adj   n

___
15

1) Black Americans give the United States their gifts (in all areas) (of American culture).

   adj   n   av adj   n   pp   adj   n

___
9

2) Black writers touch our hearts (with their stories).

   adj   n   av pp adj   n pp   n pp n

___
13

3) Black soldiers come (to America's aid) (in times) (of war).

   adj   n pp adj   n   av pp art   n pp adj   n

___
15

4) Show business (in this country) benefits (from the talents) (of Black entertainers).

   adj   n   av pro n pp adj   n

___
9

5) Black poets write us poems (of great beauty).

   art   n pp adj adj   n   av   art adj   n pp   pn

___
14

6) The talents (of great Black athletes) enrich the sports scene (in America).

   adj   n   av   art n pp adj adj   n

___
10

7) American history contains the names (of many Black patriots).

   art   n pp adj   pn   av pro adj   adj   n

___
11

8) The ranks (of Black Americans) give us countless dedicated educators.

   n pp n   av   adv pp adj   n pp   adj   n

___
14

9) People (of color) contribute greatly (to all walks) (of American life).

   pn   av   pp art   n   pp adj adj adj   n

___
12

10) America prospers (from the contributions) (of all her cultural groups).

___
122

Directions

Write what job the underlined words are doing in each sentence. Choose your answers from among the following:

subject	*direct object*	*indirect object*
object of the preposition	*verb*	*modifier*

5 points each

Sentence #	Word	Job
1	United States	*indirect object*
2	stories	*object of the preposition*
3	America's	*modifier*
4	business	*subject*
5	us	*indirect object*
6	scene	*direct object*
7	contains	*verb*
8	educators	*direct object*
9	greatly	*modifier*
10	groups	*object of the preposition*

50

Diagrams

Enter score from diagramming solutions here.

71

Total Points $\dfrac{194}{243} = 80\%$
243

Lesson 8
Linking Verbs and Sentence Patterns 4 & 5

Instructor Notes

In this lesson, linking verbs are introduced. This concept can be tricky for students to master. The Process Chart is extremely helpful, but students are occasionally resistant to using it. This lesson introduces the final step in The Process, so it's important to have them continue using it and verbalizing the steps for the first few practice sentences. The questions asked in each step help to identify the job that each part of speech is doing. This makes diagramming much easier and illustrates the logical, grammatical construction of a sentence.

This lesson provides the completed Process Chart—there are no more steps to add, only variations of some concepts they have already learned. As they continue to use The Process, the steps will become so automatic to them that they will no longer need the chart, but during the learning process, this chart gives them a solid frame to build on.

Lesson 8: Linking Verbs and Sentence Patterns 4 & 5

We have learned three sentence patterns that all use action verbs. Now we will learn about a different kind of verb: the **linking verb**.

> **Linking verbs**
> A **linking verb** is a verb that establishes a connection between its subject and a complement in the **predicate**. The **complement** can be either a noun or pronoun that is another name for the subject, or it can be an adjective that describes the subject.

Here is the difference between action verbs and linking verbs:

> **James walked down the street.**

The subject of this sentence is James. And James **did** something in the sentence: he walked.

Now, look at this sentence:

> **James seemed sleepy today.**

The subject is still James, but James isn't **doing** anything in this sentence. Instead, he is **being** something: *sleepy.*

Always Linking Verbs	Sometimes Linking Verbs	
be (is, are, am, was were, being, been)	**smell**	**stay**
seem	**taste**	**appear**
become	**look**	**sound**
	feel	**grow**

Some of these verbs are always linking verbs, such as all forms of *be, seem* and *become*, but most of them can act as action verbs, too. All of the verbs that have to do with your senses can be linking verbs.

> **Tip:** There are a couple of ways to help you figure out if a verb is acting as a linking verb. The first is to substitute it with a form of *be*. If you can do that and the sentence still makes sense, it is almost definitely acting as a linking verb. Another way to check is to replace the verb with an equals sign. If you can do that, you know that the two nouns are "equals" and you have a linking verb!

Example A: Jasmine *feels* ill.   Jasmine *is* ill.

Poor Jasmine! This sentence still makes sense and means almost the same thing. *Feels* is doing the **linking verb** job.

Example B: Paolo *smells* dinner.   Paolo *is* dinner.

Oh dear, surely not! In this sentence, *smells* is doing the **action verb** job.

The test above works most of the time. To be absolutely sure it's a linking verb, though, you must determine if it's in a linking verb sentence pattern.

Sentence Pattern 4: N-LV-N

The first linking verb pattern is called "noun – linking verb – noun," or N-LV-N The first noun or pronoun is the **subject**. Next comes the **linking verb**, followed by the second noun, which is the **predicate nominative**. The most important thing to remember is that **the subject and predicate nominative are always the same person or thing.**

> **Predicate nominative**
> A **predicate nominative** is a noun or pronoun in the predicate that renames or restates the subject. It follows a **linking verb**.

                          adj   n   lv art   n   pp art   pn

Example: My cousin is a captain (in the Navy).

Let's strip the sentence of modifiers and see what's left:

cousin – is – captain

Notice that *cousin* and *captain* are the same person in this sentence. If the sentence said, "My cousin *married* a captain in the Navy," that wouldn't be the case; the *cousin* and the *captain* are two different people. *Married* is an action verb and can only have direct and indirect objects. *Is* is a linking verb that links the predicate nominative back to the subject and can only have a complement.

Here's how we diagram Sentence Pattern 4:

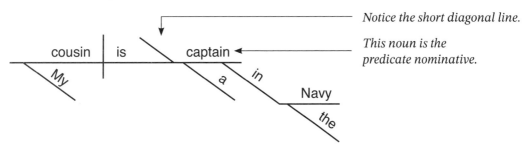

Notice the short diagonal line.

This noun is the predicate nominative.

Notice how the baseline is different from a Pattern 2 sentence with a direct object. You remember that the line separating an action verb from its direct object is vertical. In this pattern, however, the line separating the linking verb from the predicate nominative is diagonal, slanting back toward the subject.

> **Complement** comes from the same root word as **complete**. The predicate nominative or predicate adjective **completes** the subject by telling more about it.

Sentence Pattern 5: N-LV-ADJ

This is the second linking verb pattern, and the last of the five basic sentence patterns. It is called "noun – linking verb – adjective." This sentence pattern is similar to Pattern 4, except that instead of a predicate nominative (noun), there is a **predicate adjective** that describes the subject.

> **Predicate adjective**
> A **predicate adjective** is an adjective that follows a **linking verb** and describes the subject. It is a kind of complement.

Here's an example of a sentence with a predicate adjective:

> art   n   lv   adj   pp   art   adj   n
> The   students looked angry (about the   pop   quiz).

When we strip out all the modifiers, we are left with:

students – looked – angry

Using the questions from Step 2 of The Process Chart, we ask, "*which students*?" Who is *angry* describing? The answer is "*angry students.*" Because **students** is the subject but **angry** is in the predicate, we know that **looked** is acting as a linking verb and **angry** is a **predicate adjective**.

Sentence Pattern 5 is diagrammed with the same diagonal line as Pattern 4:

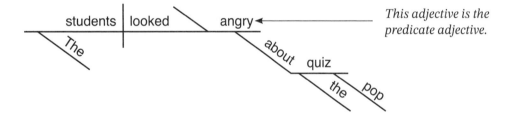

This adjective is the predicate adjective.

> We have already learned about the difference between **action verbs** (*av*) and **verbals** (*v*). Now we are adding **linking verbs** (*lv*).
>
> There's a reason that Step 5 asks you to simply mark everything that looks like a verb with a *v*. Steps 6-9 will help you to identify the main verb in the sentence as either an action verb or linking verb and add the appropriate tag. The questions asked in these steps will help you to identify the jobs of any nouns or adjectives in the predicate at the same time.
>
> Remember:
>
> • If you have an **action verb** in your sentence, then you have either Pattern 1, Pattern 2, or Pattern 3.
>
> • **Direct objects** and **indirect objects** must have an **action verb**.
>
> • If you have a **linking verb** in your sentence, then you have either Pattern 4 or Pattern 5.
>
> • **Predicate nominatives** or **predicate adjectives** must have a **linking verb**.

The Process

The Process Chart is now complete; there are no more steps to be added. If you follow the steps in order, you will find that The Process makes even complicated sentences easy!

Step 1. Find and mark all the nouns (***n***) and proper nouns (***pn***) in the sentence.
Step 2. Find and mark all the articles (***art***) and adjectives (***adj***) in the sentence.
Step 3. Find and mark all the pronouns (***pro***).
Step 4. Find and mark all the prepositions (***pp***). Put parentheses around all prepositional phrases.
Step 5. Find all words that look like verbs and mark them ***v***.
Step 6. Ask, "who or what (verb)?"

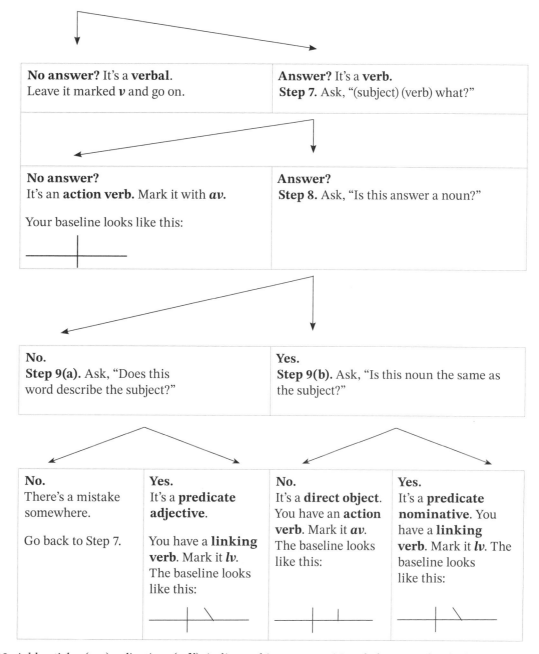

| **No answer?** It's a **verbal.** Leave it marked ***v*** and go on. | **Answer?** It's a **verb.** **Step 7.** Ask, "(subject) (verb) what?" |

| **No answer?** It's an **action verb.** Mark it with ***av***. Your baseline looks like this: | **Answer?** **Step 8.** Ask, "Is this answer a noun?" |

| **No.** **Step 9(a).** Ask, "Does this word describe the subject?" | **Yes.** **Step 9(b).** Ask, "Is this noun the same as the subject?" |

| **No.** There's a mistake somewhere. Go back to Step 7. | **Yes.** It's a **predicate adjective.** You have a **linking verb.** Mark it ***lv***. The baseline looks like this: | **No.** It's a **direct object.** You have an **action verb.** Mark it ***av***. The baseline looks like this: | **Yes.** It's a **predicate nominative.** You have a **linking verb.** Mark it ***lv***. The baseline looks like this: |

Step 10. Add articles (***art***), adjectives (***adj***), indirect objects, prepositional phrases, adverbs (***adv***), and conjunctions (***conj***)* to the diagram.

Step 11. Congratulate yourself! You've successfully parsed and diagrammed the whole sentence!

* Conjunctions are taught in Lesson 10. Don't worry about parsing or diagramming them until then.

Sentence Patterns 4 & 5: Exercise A

Directions

All of the sentences in this exercise are either Pattern 4 or Pattern 5; that is, they will have a linking verb and a complement, either a predicate nominative or a predicate adjective. Parse and then diagram each sentence. Use your Process Chart to work through the steps and figure out which pattern you have. Stripping the sentence of all modifiers can help you identify the parts of speech that will determine the pattern. Remember to use your notes and The Process Chart if you need any help.

    adj   *pn*   *lv*   *adj*   *n*   *pp*   *adj*   *n*

1) Jewish Americans are important <u>contributors</u> (to American culture).

    ——*pn*—— *lv* *pro* *pp*   *adj*   *adv*   *adj*   *n*

2) George Burns was one (of America's most beloved <u>comedians</u>).

    art   *adv*   *adj*   ——*pn*—— *lv* *art* *adj*   *adj*   *n*

3) The <u>extremely</u> talented Barbra Streisand is a famous popular singer.

    ——*pn*——   *lv*   *adj*   *adj*   ——*pn*—— *pp* *art* *adj*   *n*

4) Henry Kissinger <u>remained</u> America's powerful Secretary of State (during the Nixon administration).

    adj   *adj*   ——*adj*——   *n*   *lv*   ——*pn*——

5) One influential Jewish-American publisher was <u>Joseph Pulitzer</u>.

    ——*adj*—— *adj*   *n*   *lv*   *adv*   *adj*

6) Dr. Jonas Salk's polio <u>vaccine</u> was terribly important.

    ——*adj*—— *n*   *lv*   *adv*   *adj*   *pp* *adj*   *pro*

7) Albert Einstein's mind appeared more <u>brilliant</u> (than any other).

    art   ——*adj*——   ——*pn*—   *lv*   *adv*   *adj* *pp* *art*   *n*

8) The Baseball Hall of Fame's Sandy Koufax seemed greatly feared (as a pitcher).

    ——*adv*—— *n*   *lv*   *adv*   *adj*

9) George Gershwin's music was incredibly beautiful.

    art *n* *pp* *adj*   *n*   *lv*   *adv*   *adj*

10) The history (of Jewish <u>Americans</u>) is indeed remarkable.

Directions

Write which job the underlined word is doing in each sentence. Choose your answers from among the following:

subject	predicate nominative	predicate adjective
object of the preposition	modifier	verb

Sentence #	Word	Job
1	contributors	*predicate nominative*
2	comedians	*object of the preposition*
3	extremely	*modifier*
4	remained	*verb*
5	Joseph Pulitzer	*predicate nominative*
6	vaccine	*subject*
7	brilliant	*predicate adjective*
10	Americans	*object of the preposition*

Sentence Patterns 4 & 5: Exercise B

Directions

All of the sentences in this exercise are either Pattern 4 or Pattern 5; that is, they will have a linking verb and a complement. Parse and then diagram each sentence. Use your Process Chart to work through the steps.

       art adj   n   lv   adj   pp art   n   pp art adj   adj   n

1) The young girl was terrified (by the <u>guns</u>) (of the Nazi prison guards).

       art   n   pp adj   n   lv   n   pp art   adj   adj   n

2) The members (of her family) became <u>prisoners</u> (of the anti-Jewish German government)

       pp art   adj   pn

(in the early 1940s).

       ——pn——   lv art   adj   n   pp   ——pn——   pp   pn

3) <u>Riva Minska</u> was a helpless inmate (of Camp Mittelsteine) (in Germany).

       art   adj   adj   n   pp adj   n   lv   pro*

4) The prisoner identification number (on her arm) was <u>55082</u>.

* While students have learned that all numbers are pronouns, this number has particular significance due to its purpose. They may choose to mark it with /n/ or even /pn/ and be correct.

       pn   lv   adj   pp   n

5) Riva <u>grew</u> weak (from hunger).

       adj adj   n   lv   adv   adj pp adj   n

6) This young girl felt desperately <u>lonely</u> (for her parents).

       pro   lv   n   pp art adj   n   pp art adj   n

7) They remained prisoners (in a death camp) (in a <u>different</u> place).

       art   n   pp adj   n   lv   adv   adv   adj

8) The guards (at Riva's <u>camp</u>) were almost unbelievably cruel.

       art adj   n   pp   n   lv   adj

9) The mere idea (of escape) looked <u>hopeless.</u>

                    pn   lv   adv   adj   pp   art   adj   n   pp   adj   n

10) Riva <u>felt</u> less miserable (in the secret world) (of her poetry).

Directions

Write what job the underlined words are doing in each sentence. Choose your answers from among the following:

subject   *predicate nominative*   *predicate adjective*

object of the preposition   *modifier*   *verb*

Sentence #	Word	Job
1	guns	*object of the preposition*
2	prisoners	*predicate nominative*
3	Riva Minska	*subject*
4	55082	*predicate nominative*
5	grew	*verb*
6	lonely	*predicate adjective*
7	different	*modifier*
8	camp	*object of the preposition*
9	hopeless	*predicate adjective*
10	felt	*verb*

Sentence Patterns 4 & 5: Exercise C

Directions

The sentences below may be any one of the five sentence patterns you have learned: N-V, N-V-N, N-V-N-N, N-LV-N, and N-LV-ADJ. Use The Process Chart to parse and diagram each sentence.

art   adj   n   pp   pn   pp   pn   av   pp   pn   pp   ————pn————   pp   pn

1) The first group (of Jews) (in America) <u>came</u> (from Brazil) (to New Amsterdam) (in 1654).

art   adj   adj   n   pp   art   adj   n   lv   art   n   pp   pn

2) The second Jewish <u>settlement</u> (in the American colonies) was the <u>village</u> (of Newport)

pp   ————pn————   pp   pn

(in Rhode Island) (in 1658).

pn   lv   art   adj   n   ————pp————   adj   adj   n

3) Jews were "an alien nation," (according to <u>some</u> ignorant settlers).

art   adj   pn   pp   pn   av   pp   art   ————pn————   pp   art

4) The <u>first</u> Jews (in Pennsylvania) traded (with the Native Americans) (along the

————pn————   pp   pn

Delaware River) (in 1655).

art   adj   pn   pp   pn   av   pro   art   adv   adj   n   pp   pn

5) The devout Jews (of Philadelphia) built <u>themselves</u> a very beautiful <u>synagogue</u> (in 1770).

pp   art   n   pp   art   ————pn————   adv   adj   pn   av   pp   art

6) (At the time) (of the American Revolution), approximately 2,500 Jews lived (in the

adj   n

American colonies).

adj   adj   adj   n   lv   adv   adj   pp   art   n   pp   adj   n

7) This tiny Jewish <u>minority</u> became historically important (during the days) (of our fight)

pp   n   pp   ————pn————

(for freedom) (from Great Britain).

pn   av   art   adj   n   pp   art   adj   n   pp   art   n

8) Jews played an <u>important</u> part (in the revolutionary struggle) (from the start).

pn   pp   pn   adv   av   pp   art   n   pp   n

9) Jews (from Europe) also joined (in the fight) (for freedom).

lv   adj   pp   adj   adj   adj   n

10) Be <u>proud</u> (of these early Jewish patriots)!

Directions

Write what job the underlined words are doing in each sentence. Choose your answers from among the following:

subject	*direct object*	*indirect object*	*predicate nominative*
object of the preposition	*modifier*	*predictae adjective*	*verb*

Sentence #	Word	Job
1	came	*verb*
2	settlement	*subject*
2	village	*predicate nominative*
3	some	*modifier*
4	first	*modifier*
5	themselves	*indirect object*
5	synagogue	*direct object*
7	minority	*subject*
8	important	*modifier*
10	proud	*predicate adjective*

Application & Enrichment

Comma Splits

Commas are very important, often misunderstood punctuation marks. Using them correctly (or incorrectly!) makes a great difference in how easily your reader understands what you have written. You've learned a bit about fixing comma splices (in the Lesson 4 Application & Enrichment activity). Now you know enough grammar to learn about another common error that trips up readers.

We know that a comma means a pause in the flow of the text. When we see a comma, our mind naturally pauses in our reading. That's great when it's a properly placed comma, in a place where you want the reader to naturally pause. But when commas are in the wrong place, text lurches along like it is gasping for breath. Commas randomly placed in sentences are called **comma splits.**

Comma split

This is the opposite of a comma splice. Rather than incorrectly joining two sentences, a **comma split** incorrectly divides a sentence. It is a single comma that comes between two words, phrases, or clauses that shouldn't be separated. Here is a list of places a comma should never be:

1) There should never be **only one** comma between the **subject** and **verb**.

   Example:
   Incorrect: The butler carrying a tray, walked into the room.
   Correct: The butler, carrying a tray, walked into the room.
   Also correct: Carrying a tray, the butler walked into the room.

2) There should never be **only one** comma separating a **verb** and its **direct object**.

   Example:
   Incorrect: We discovered after searching carefully, many things.
   Correct: We discovered, after searching carefully, many things.
   Also correct: After searching carefully, we discovered many things.
   Or: We discovered many things after searching carefully.

3) There should never be **only one** comma separating a **linking verb** and its **predicate adjective** or **predicate nominative** (also known as its **complement**).

   Example:
   Incorrect: James felt, absolutely wonderful.
   Correct: James felt absolutely wonderful.

4) There should never be **only one** comma separating a **modifier** and its **noun**. If there is more than one adjective, there should be no comma after the final adjective before the noun.

   Example:
   Incorrect: The soft, cuddly, sweater was gorgeous.
   Correct: The soft, cuddly sweater was gorgeous.

5) There should never be **only one** comma separating a **verb** and its **indirect object**.

   Example:
   Incorrect: I wrote, my aunt in Florida a letter.
   Correct: I wrote my aunt in Florida a letter.

6) There should never be **only one** comma separating an **indirect object** and its **direct object**.

Example:
Incorrect: I wrote my aunt in Florida, a letter.
Correct: I wrote my aunt in Florida a letter.

Always know **why** you are placing a comma in a sentence. Remember that nonessential information in the middle of a sentence needs to have commas on both ends. And remember the no-no splits!

1) subject and verb

2) verb and direct object

3) linking verb and complement

4) modifier and its noun

5) verb and indirect object

6) indirect object and direct object

Directions
The following sentences all contain comma splits. Using the list above, write what is being split by the comma.

Example: The football player, was tired from practice.

splits subject (player) and verb (was)

1) Joey threw him, the ball.
    splits indirect object (him) *and direct object* (ball)

2) The orange, cat slept in the sun.
    splits modifier (orange) *and its noun* (cat)

3) I read, my little cousin the book about dinosaurs.
    splits verb (read) *and indirect object* (cousin)

4) Pudge Heffelfinger was, the first professional American football player.
    splits linking verb (was) *and predicate nominative* (player)

5) The boy tossed, the ball back to the umpire.
    splits verb (tossed) *and direct object* (ball)

Sentence Patterns 4 & 5: Assessment

Directions

The sentences below may be any one of the five sentence patterns you have learned. Use The Process Chart to parse and diagram each sentence.

Each correctly identified word or prepositional phrase is worth one point.

          adj   *n*   *lv* *art*   *adj*   *n*   *pp*   *n*   *pp*   *adj*   *n*

__ **1)** Head coverings are a traditional <u>symbol</u> (of modesty) (in Jewish culture).
13

         pp   *adj*   *adj*   *adj*   *n*   *n*   *av*   *adj*   *n*   *pp*   *n*

__ **2)** (In many orthodox Jewish communities,) <u>women</u> wear head coverings (in public)
16

         pp   *n*

(after marriage).

         adj   *adj*   *n*   *av*   *adj* *adj*   *n*   *pp* *art*   *n*

__ **3)** Some Jewish women hide their <u>own</u> hair (under a wig).
11

         pro   *av* *art*   *adj*   *adj*   *n*   *pp*   *adj*   *adj*   ——*adj*——   *n*

__ **4)** Others wear a knotted head scarf (like other traditional Middle Eastern <u>cultures</u>).
12

         adj   *n*   *av* *adv*   *pro*   *pp*   *n*

__ **5)** These traditions go back <u>thousands</u> (of years).
8

         art   *adj*   *n*   *pp* *adj*   *n*   *av*   *adj*   *n*   *pp* *adj*   *n*

__ **6)** The traditional clothing (of many cultures) includes some <u>kind</u> (of hair covering).
14

         n   *lv* *art* *adj*   *n*   *pp*   *adj*   *n*   *adv*

__ **7)** Scarves are a fashion <u>choice</u> (for many wearers) today.
10

         art   *adj*   *n*   *lv*   *adv*   *adj*   *pp*   *adj*   *n*

__ **8)** The luxurious fabrics are beautifully <u>embroidered</u> (with intricate patterns).
10

         n   *pp*   *n*   *av*   *n*   *n*   *pp* *adj*   *n*

__ **9)** Layers (of scarves) provide <u>people</u> warmth (in cold climates).
11

$$\text{adj} \quad n \quad av \quad adj \quad n \quad pp \quad adj \quad n \quad pp \quad art \quad n$$

__ **10)** Head coverings <u>serve</u> many purposes (in different communities) (around the world).
13

══
118

Directions

Write what job the underlined words are doing in each sentence. Choose your answers from among the following:

subject	*direct object*	*indirect object*	*predicate nominative*
object of the preposition	*modifier*	*predictae adjective*	*verb*

Five points each

Sentence #	Word	Job
1	symbol	*predicate nominative*
2	women	*subject*
3	own	*modifier*
4	cultures	*object of the preposition*
5	thousands	*direct object*
6	kind	*direct object*
7	choice	*predicate nominative*
8	embroidered	*predicate adjective*
9	people	*indirect object*
10	serve	*verb*

══
50

Diagrams

Enter score from diagramming solutions here.

$$\frac{\overline{\quad\quad}}{81}$$

$$\frac{199}{249} = 80\%$$

$$\frac{\overline{\quad\quad}}{249}\text{Total Points}$$

Lesson 9
Helping Verbs

Instructor Notes

This lesson introduces helping verbs, those verbs that are used to form different tenses. Some of these verbs are familiar as linking verbs, and some can stand alone as action verbs. Students should become familiar with these verbs so that they do not confuse them with adverbs.

Verb phrases with helping verbs are diagrammed in the same way as single verbs, so students find it a relatively easy lesson as long as they familiarize themselves with these helping verbs.

Lesson 9: Helping Verbs

In this lesson, we will study **helping verbs**. To begin, we need to remember the definition of a **phrase**:

> **Phrases**
> A phrase is a group of words that works together as a unit to express a concept.

Helping verbs come before action verbs or linking verbs to create a **verb phrase**. They "help" by creating different tenses: past, future, conditional, and so on. In other programs, helping verbs are sometimes called auxiliary verbs. Using helping verbs changes what we know about the action of the main verb.

Example 1:   Main verb   crawl

Verb phrase   will crawl   (*will* is the helping verb)

If we use this verb phrase in a sentence, what does it tell you about the action?

The baby *will crawl.*

Is the baby crawling right now? No. The baby will crawl at some point *in the future.*

Example 2:   Main verb   listen

Verb phrase   has been listening   (*has* and *been* are the helping verbs)

Here is the verb phrase in a sentence:

Juan *has been listening* to a lot of podcasts.

What do we know from this particular phrase? Juan started listening to podcasts at some point in the past, and he is still listening to a lot of podcasts. It shows a continuous, or **progressive**, action. If we took away the helping verbs, it would change the meaning slightly:

Juan *listens* to a lot of podcasts.

In this sentence, without the helping verbs, we know that Juan listens to podcasts, but we lose the fact that this is a change in his behavior—that he previously did not listen to podcasts, but at some point he started listening, and he still does. Without the helping verbs, we don't know as much about when Juan started listening.

> We'll talk more about how helping verbs create verb tenses in upcoming Application & Enrichment activities.

Example 3:   Main verb   find

Verb phrase   would have been found   (*would, have,* and *been* are the helping verbs)

Let's use this verb phrase in a sentence:

The keys *would have been found*.

Have the keys been found? No. What word tells us that, specifically? ***Would***. If we remove that word, the remaining helping verbs say the opposite. ***Would*** is an example of a **modal**, which is a helping verb that makes the action or linking verb **conditional**. That means that the action of the main verb is not a done deal—it is only hypothetical. Something else would need to happen before the action becomes reality. In our example sentence, we can add a condition to the end to illustrate this:

The keys would have been found *if we had looked under the mat*.

If we had looked under the mat...did we look under the mat? No, but *if* we **had**, we would have found the keys. That's the condition that is implied by using **would** in this sentence.

So you can see that using helping verbs adds a whole range of meaning to our sentences beyond what a simple action or linking verb can provide!

Here is a list of verbs that can do the helping verb job. You should become very familiar with these verbs:

to be:	to have:	The Modals
is	has	will
am	have	would
are	had	shall
was		should
were	**to do:**	can
be	do	could
being	does	may
been	did	might
		must

You'll notice that some of the verbs listed as sometimes helping verbs can also be **action verbs,** such as ***have*** and ***do***. If one of these verbs is the ***last*** verb in a verb phrase, it is doing the job of an **action verb.** If it is ***not*** the last verb in a verb phrase, it is doing the job of a **helping verb.**

Example 4:

pro hv av adj   n

I will do my homework.   (*will do* is the verb phrase and *do* is an action verb)

pro hv adv   av   adj   n

I do not* want any lunch.   (*do want* is the verb phrase and *do* is a helping verb)

*__Not__ is always an adverb that negates, or flips, the verb to mean the opposite.

There are also verbs on the helping verbs list above that you have learned as linking verbs (all the forms of the verb **to be**). If they are the ***last*** verb in the verb phrase, they are doing the job of a **linking verb**. If they are anywhere else in the verb phrase, they are doing the job of a **helping verb**.

Example 5:

pn   hv   lv   art   n

John will be* a senior.   (*will be* is the verb phrase and *be* is a linking verb)

pn   hv   av   pp   n

John is going (to college).   (*is going* is the verb phrase and *is* (a form of *to be*) is a helping verb)

*__Be__ is always the form of ***to be*** that's used as a linking verb if there is a helping verb, no matter what the subject is.

Note: A favorite spot for adverbs to hide is between a helping verb and the main verb (*I should **really** do my homework*). That's why it's so useful to be familiar with the helping verbs—otherwise, you might mistake an adverb for a helping verb or vice versa.

How to diagram helping verbs

Helping verbs are just part of the verb phrase, so they are diagrammed together with the main verb like this:

Example 6:

pn   hv   lv adj   adj   n   pp   adj   n

Josephine will be my study partner (in algebra class).

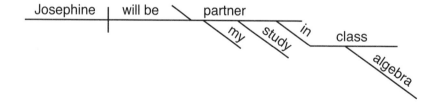

How to diagram questions

Most of the questions in English are formed by rearranging the words in a statement and putting them in a different order. Look at the following examples:

Example 7:   **Statement:**   I should do my homework.

Question: Should I do my homework?

To form the question, the helping verb is moved in front of the subject. To diagram a question, the helping verb(s) and main verb still go in the verb position. The first word of the sentence should be capitalized to show that it came first in the sentence.

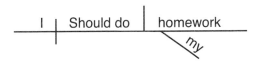

Example 8:   **Statement:**   He walked to school.

Question: Did he walk to school?

In Example 8, because there was no helping verb in the statement, one was added to make the question. But again, it comes in front of the subject.

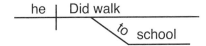

Helping Verbs: Exercise A

Directions

Parse and diagram the sentences. Be on the lookout for adverbs hiding inside verb phrases! Use The Process Chart and your notes for help. Diagramming solutions are found after the index.

————————pn———————   hv   av   pp   pn   pp   pn

1) Santha Rama Rau was born (in India) (in 1923).

————pn————   hv   adv   lv   adj   pp   adj   adj   n

2) Rama Rau has long been famous (for her superb essays).

pro   hv   hv   lv   adv   adj   pp   adj   n   pp   adj   n

3) She could have been well known (for her writings) (beyond her essays).

pro   hv   adv   hv   lv   adj   pp   adj   n   adv

4) She could easily have been popular (for her novels), also.

pp   ————————pn————————   pro   hv   av   art   adj   n   pp   pn

5) (In "By Any Other Name,") she has portrayed the cultural conflict (in India)

——pp——   art   adj   n

(because of the English colonization).

hv   pro   av   pro   pp   adj   n

6) Do you know anything (about cultural conflicts)?

adj   n   hv   av   pro   pp   art   n   pp   adj   n

7) This essay might help you (to an understanding) (of such conflicts).

adj   adj   n   hv   av   pp   art   n   pp   adj   n

8) Two Indian sisters were sent (to a school) (for English children).

        art   *adj*   *n*   *hv*   *hv*   *av*   *pp*   *adj*   *n*   *pp*   *n*

9) The Anglo-Indian school had been taught (by British teachers) (for years).

        adj   *adj*   *n*   *hv*   *hv*   *av*   *adj*   *adj*   *n*   *pp* *adj* *adj*   *n*

10) This British-run school must have caused many cultural problems (for its Indian students).

Helping Verbs: Exercise B

Directions

Parse and diagram the sentences below. Look out for adverbs. Use The Process Chart and your notes if you need help. Diagramming solutions are found after the index.

    art   *n*   *hv*   *hv*   *av*   *adj*   *adj*   *adj*   *n*   *pp* *adj*   *n*

1)   The sisters had been given two beautiful <u>Indian</u> names (by their parents).

    pp *art* *adj* *n* *pp*   *n*   *art*   *n*   *hv*   *av*   *adj*   *n*   *pp*   *adj*   *n*

2)   (On the first day)(of school), the <u>teacher</u> had indicated her helplessness (with Indian names).

    adj   *adj*   *name*   *hv*   *lv*   *pn*

3)   Santha's new name would be <u>Cynthia</u>.

    pn   *hv*   *hv*   *av*   *pp*   *pn*

4)   Premila would be known (as <u>Pamela</u>).

    art   *n*   *hv* *adv*   *av*   *art*   *n*   *pp* *adj* *adj*   *n*

5)   The girls could not understand the reason (for these <u>new</u> names).

    pro   *hv*   *adv*   *av*   *art*   *n*   *pp* *adj*   *adj*   *n*   *pp* *adj* *adj*

6)   They would soon understand the <u>reasons</u> (for their mother's anxiety)(about this new

    adj   *n*

English school).

    adj *adj*   *adj*   *n*   *hv* *hv*   *av*   *pp* *art* *adj*   *n*   *pp* *art* *adj*   *n*

7)   <u>Four</u> other Indian children had been assigned (to the same class)(with the two sisters).

    pro *pp* *art* *adj*   *n*   *hv*   *av*   *art* *adj*   *n*   ——*pp*—— *adj* *adj*   *adj*   *n*

8)   One (of the other girls)(was wearing a cotton dress (instead of her native Indian <u>clothes</u>).

    art n hv av adj   n   pp art   n   pp adj   n

9) The girls <u>would ask</u> their mother (about the possibility)(of English-style dresses)

    pp   pro

(for themselves).

    hv pro av art adj   n pp adj   n   pp adj   n

10) Did <u>they</u> have a good reason (for their desire) (for different clothes)?

Fill in the blank

11) Helping verbs are verbs that come _____ the main verb and help form different _____ .

   before, tenses

12) Adjectives are words that _____ .

   modify nouns and pronouns

13) A pronoun is a word that _____ .

   takes the place of a noun

14) The helping verb(s) and the main verb together make up the _____ .

   verb phrase

Directions

Write what job the underlined word is doing in each sentence. Choose your answers from among the following:

| subject | direct object | object of the preposition | verb |
| indirect object | predicate nominative | predicate adjective | modifier |

Sentence #	Word	Job
1	Indian	*modifier*
2	teacher	*subject*
3	Cynthia	*predicate nominative*
4	Pamela	*object of the preposition*
5	new	*modifier*
6	reasons	*direct object*
7	Four	*modifier*
8	clothes	*object of the preposition*
9	would ask	*verb*
10	They	*subject*

Helping Verbs: Exercise C

Directions

Parse and diagram the sentences below. Diagramming solutions are found after the index.

        adj   adj   n   pp   n   hv   lv   adv   adj   pp art adj   n
1) That first <u>day</u> (of school) had been very difficult (for the two sisters).

           pn   hv   hv   av   pp art   n   pp adj adj   n
2) Santha <u>had been asked</u> (by the teacher) (for her new name).

        pro   hv   adv   av   pro
3) She could not remember <u>it</u>!

        art   n   pp art   n   hv   av   pp pro
4) The rest (of the <u>class</u>) had laughed (at her).

        pro   hv   lv   art adv   adj   n
5) She had been a very embarrassed <u>girl</u>!

        pp   n   art adj   adj   n   hv   av   n   ——pp——   adj   adj   n
6) (At <u>lunchtime</u>,) the other Indian students were eating sandwiches (instead of normal Indian food).

        pp   n   pro hv   adv   av   art   adj   n
7) (At recess,) she could not understand the competitive <u>games</u>.

        pp   n   art   n   hv   hv   av   n   pp adj   n   pp adj   n
8) (At home,) the <u>girls</u> had been taught kindness (to younger children) (in their games).

        adj   adj   n   hv adv   av   art   adj   n
9) These English children did not return the <u>same</u> courtesy!

art adj n   hv lv adj pp art n pp n   pp adj adj n

10) The two sisters would feel <u>glad</u> (at the close) (of school) (on that first day).

Fill in the blank

11) An antecedent is_____.

the noun the pronoun stands for

12) In a *noun – linking verb – noun* sentence pattern, the second noun is called

the _____.

predicate nominative

13) List the modifiers in this sentence. _____

the, this, in this sentence

14) The verb phrase is made up of the _____.

helping verb(s) and main verb

Directions

Write what job each underlined word is doing in the sentence. Choose your answers from among the following:

| subject | direct object | object of the preposition | verb |
| indirect object | predicate nominative | predicate adjective | modifier |

Sentence #	Word	Job
1	day	*subject*
2	had been asked	*verb*
3	it	*direct object*
4	class	*object of the preposition*
5	girl	*predicate nominative*
6	lunchtime	*object of the preposition*
7	games	*direct object*
8	girls	*subject*
9	same	*modifier*
10	glad	*predicate adjective*

Application & Enrichment

Synonyms Activity 4

We've described synonyms and modifiers as adding "spice and flavor" to our writing. But, just like eating too much ice cream can give you a stomach ache, too many synonyms, adjectives, or adverbs can detract from your message. Readers can get lost trying to follow your words if there are too many or they're too complicated.

So how much description is enough? That's a matter of personal preference, as a writer, but there are some guidelines you can follow to help you decide.

1) Use synonyms that your reader will understand.

> The secondary interlocutor impeded evolution of our colloquy to achieve congruity.

Huh? This sentence is packed with fancy synonyms, but it doesn't make much sense!

Try this one:
> The other speaker stopped the progress of our conversation toward agreement.

Now we can understand it, but it's still a little awkward. Let's think about what we're trying to say and try again:

> The other speaker stopped us from reaching an agreement.

Much better and clearer! Good writing should not be complicated or confusing. We need to take care not to use fancy words just because we can. Every word we choose needs to have a purpose in our sentence.

2) Coco Chanel, known as one of the most elegant women who ever lived, gave the following advice about jewelry: "Before leaving the house, look in the mirror and take one thing off." This is great advice when we look at our descriptive sentences, too. Are all of the synonyms we are using adding to the word picture we want to paint? What about the modifiers we've added—are they all essential to the picture? Are there any repetitive words that can be removed? Look closely at your sentence. Is there anything you can take off without losing the meaning?

Here's a puffed-up sentence with lots of descriptors:

> The wizened, bent, unkempt, messy old woman happily, peacefully lived with her bony, skinny, toothless cat in her small, tiny, cramped, cozy cottage.

If we look at each noun and adjective with its modifiers, there are some words with very similar meanings that can be eliminated. Let's look at the first noun phrase:

The wizened, bent, unkempt, messy old woman

Wizened and *bent* mean almost the same thing; choose one to keep. The same is true of *unkempt* and *messy*; again, choose just one. *Old*, however, is on its own, and none of our other modifiers say that, so we should keep it. Write your new noun phrase on the line below:

Answers will vary. One possible answer is given.

The wizened, unkempt old woman

Next we have a verb phrase with some adverbs:
happily, peacefully lived

While *happily* and *peacefully* don't mean the same thing, they don't really add a lot to the sentence together. We would get the same mental image with only one or the other. Choose one of the adverbs to keep, and write your new verb phrase below:

Answers will vary. One possible answer is given.

———————————————————————————————————————

happily lived

Look at the next noun phrase: *bony, skinny, toothless cat.* What can you take out of the phrase but still paint the proper mental picture?

Answers will vary. One possible answer is given.

———————————————————————————————————————

skinny, toothless cat

Now do the same with the last noun phrase: *small, tiny, cramped, cozy cottage*

Answers will vary. but two to three of the following adjectives should be removed:
small, tiny, cramped, cozy.

———————————————————————————————————————

cozy cottage

Finally, put it all together by writing the simplified sentence with your new phrases below:

Answers will vary.

———————————————————————————————————————

The wizened, unkempt old woman happily lived with her skinny, toothless cat in her cozy cottage.

Your new and improved sentence should be much clearer and easier to read while losing none of the "spice and flavor" synonyms and modifiers provide.

Helping Verbs: Assessment

Directions

Parse and diagram all of the sentences below.

Each correctly identified word or prepositional phrase is worth one point.

              pp art n pp   adj   adj   n   art adj   n   hv   av   pp art adj   n

__ **1)** (On the day) (of Premila's first test), the girls' <u>lives</u> would change (in a big way).
19

               pn   hv   adv   av   pp   art n   pp   adj   n

__ **2)** Premila had suddenly marched (through the <u>door</u>) (of Santha's classroom).
12

               pro hv   av   adj   n   adv

__ **3)** "We <u>are leaving</u> this place now!"
6

               pn   hv   lv   adv   adj   pp   adj   n

__ **4)** Santha had been completely <u>dumbfounded</u> (by Premila's behavior).
9

               pro hv ·adv   av   adj   n   adv

__ **5)** She could not disobey her <u>sister</u>, however.
7

               pro hv   adv   av   adj   n   adv

__ **6)** "I can never attend <u>that</u> school again."
7

               pp   art   n   pp adj   n   pn   hv   av   pp   art   n   pp   adj

__ **7)** (On the way) (to their home), Santha was wondering (about the reason) (for their
20

        adj   n

sudden <u>departure</u>).

               pp   n   pn   hv   av pp art   n

__ **8)** (At home), <u>Mother</u> would ask (for a reason).
10

               art   adj   n   hv   av   adj art   adj   n   pp   n   pp   n

__ **9)** The British teacher <u>had accused</u> all the Indian students (of cheating) (on tests)!
15

```
      pp    adj    adj    pn       adv      adj  adj   n     hv      av    pp  art   n    pp  art
```
__ **10)** (To happy little Santha), however, this bad thing had happened (to a girl) (by the
22

```
         n    pp     pn
```
name) (of <u>Cynthia</u>)!

====
127

Fill in the blank

1 point each

__ **11)** A helping verb helps the main verb form different _____.
1
       tenses

__ **12)** A verb is not a verb unless it has a _____.
1
       subject

__ **13)** Which word in this sentence is the predicate nominative? _____.
1
       nominative

__ **14)** An adjective is a word that _____.
1
       describes or modifies a noun or pronoun

__ **15)** A pronoun is a word that _____.
1
       takes the place of a noun

__ **16)** What is an antecedent? _____.
1
       the noun the pronoun stands for

__ **17)** Which kind of noun can consist of more than one word? _____.
1
       a proper noun

__ **18)** The helping verb(s) and the main verb make up the _____.
1
       verb phrase

====
8

Directions

Write what job the underlined words are doing in each sentence. Choose your answers from among the following:

subject	*direct object*	*object of the preposition*	*verb*
indirect object	*predicate nominative*	*predicate adjective*	*modifier*

Five points each

Sentence #	Word	Job
1	lives	*subject*
2	door	*object of the preposition*
3	are leaving	*verb*
4	dumbfounded	*predicate adjective*
5	sister	*direct object*
6	that	*modifier*
7	departure	*object of the preposition*
8	Mother	*subject*
9	had accused	*verb*
10	Cynthia	*object of the preposition*

Diagrams

Enter score from diagramming solutions here.

$\overline{\overline{}}$
50

$\overline{\overline{}}$ *Total Points* $\dfrac{202}{253} = 80\%$
253

Conjunctions & Compound Situations

Instructor Notes

When students first look at their notes for this lesson, they might be intimidated. But they actually already know all of the difficult parts! The only new concepts that are introduced are how conjunctions join two (or more) of the same kinds of things, and how different conjunctions change the meaning of the sentence. A simple new diagramming mark is also introduced.

Lesson 10: Conjunctions & Compound Situations

In this lesson, we will learn about small, simple words we use every day. They're called **conjunctions**. We use them to join together words, phrases, and sentences, and they can change the meaning of what we say. Look at these sentences:

You can invite Phoebe, Sanjay, *and* Rob to the movies with you. (Three people are going to the movies with you.)

You can invite Phoebe, Sanjay, *or* Rob to the movies with you. (One person is going to the movies with you.)

What a difference can be made by changing just one little word!

Conjunctions
A conjunction is a word that joins **grammatical equals**: a noun to a noun, a verb to a verb, a phrase to a phrase, or even a sentence to a sentence.

The two (or more) things that are being joined together by the conjunction **must be the same kind of thing!**

There are three kinds of conjunctions:

- Coordinating conjunctions

- Correlative conjunctions

- Subordinating conjunctions (we'll talk about these in Level 4)

Coordinating conjunctions
A coordinating conjunction is a word that connects two or more words, sentences, phrases, or clauses. Remember, whatever items are being joined by a coordinating conjunction must be the same part of speech!

for (*when it means **because***)*

and

nor

but

or

yet (*when it means **but***)*

so

And is the most commonly used conjunction, so it's the one in most of the examples and exercises. You can remember all of these conjunctions with the acronym FANBOYS, which uses the first letter of each one.

*In today's English, *for* is usually a preposition and *yet* is usually an adverb, but if you read older or more advanced literature, you may see these words doing their conjunction jobs.

	pn	av	art	n	conj	art	n
Example 1:	Anne	cleaned	the	kitchen	and	the	bedroom.

And joins two nouns: *kitchen* and *bedroom*.

	pro	hv	av	pp	art	n	conj	pp	art	n
Example 2:	We	will	go	(to	the	store)	and	(to	the	cleaners).

And joins two prepositional phrases: *to the store* and *to the cleaners*.

Correlative conjunctions

Correlative conjunctions do the same job as coordinating conjunctions: they connect grammatical equals, whether words, phrases, or sentences. However, they will always be found in pairs with other words between.

either...or	both...and
neither...nor	not only...but (also)*

*Sometimes *also* will not be in the sentence, but it's always implied.

	pro	hv	av		art	n		art	n
Example 3:	You	can	take	either	the	pie	or	the	cake.

conj

(Notice how correlative conjunctions are parsed: underline them and draw an arrow to each; mark **conj** beneath the sentence.)

Either...or joins two nouns: *pie* and *cake*.

	art	n	lv	adj		adj	
Example 4:	The	cat	is	both	beautiful	and	smart.

conj

Both...and joins two predicate adjectives: *beautiful* and *smart*.

Now you try. What are the correlative conjunctions in the following sentences? What parts of speech do they connect?

	adj	n	pn	lv		adj		adj
	My	cat	Pumpkin	is	not only	orange	but also	round.

conj

	n		n	lv	adj	—v—	pro
	Neither	diet	nor	exercise	is	able	to	help	her.

conj

Compound Situations

A **compound situation** is when there are two (or more) of something joined by a conjunction in a sentence. All sentences that have any kind of a conjunction include a compound situation. Two or more subjects joined by a conjunction is called a **compound subject**, two or more verbs joined by a conjunction is a **compound verb**, and so on, all the way up to a **compound sentence**.

To diagram a compound situation, go to the place where that word, if it were only one word, would be diagrammed. Then you will make "branches" to add as many words or phrases as necessary. The conjunction is added on a dotted line that connects the parts of the compound situation, just like a conjunction does in a sentence. Compare the following examples:

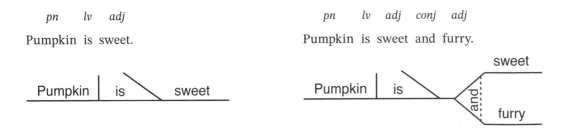

As you know, a predicate adjective is diagrammed by marking a diagonal line on the baseline between the linking verb and the predicate adjective. In the second sentence, the line branches after the diagonal because there are two predicate adjectives that both describe Pumpkin the cat.

All of the possible compound situations you might come across have been diagrammed on the following pages.

A) Compound Subject

Example:

| pn | conj | pn | av | adv |

Adam and Emma walked home.

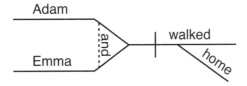

B) Compound Verb

Example 1:

| pn | hv | av | conj | av | art | n |

John was washing and waxing the car.

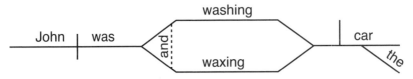

Notice that the baseline branches after *was* (which applies to both verbs) and is rejoined before the direct object *car* (which is the direct object of both verbs). Only the parts that are compounds need to be branched.

pn   av   art   n   conj   av   art   n

Example 2:   John washed the car and mowed the lawn.

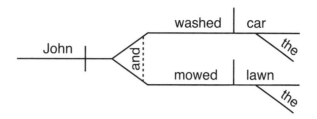

In this example, the baseline branches before the verb and does not need to be rejoined, because each verb has its own direct object, and there was nothing shared in the rest of the predicate.

C) Compound Direct Object

pn   av   art   n   conj   art   adj   n

Example: Olivia cleaned the kitchen and the living room.

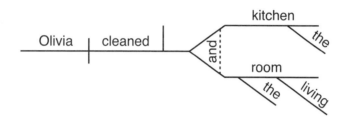

D) Compound Indirect Object

—*pn*— *av adj   n   conj pro art   n*

Example: Aunt Mia sent my brother and me a present.

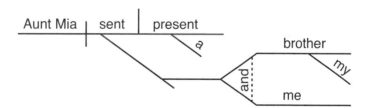

E) Compound Predicate Nominative or Predicate Adjective

pro   lv   adj   conj   adj

Example: She felt hungry and tired.

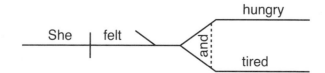

F) Compound Prepositional Phrases

Example:

pro   *av*   *pp*   *art*   *n*   *conj*   *pp*   *art*   *n*

We rode (over the river) and (through the woods).

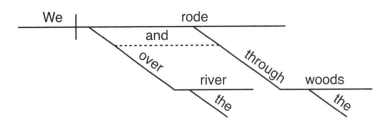

G) Prepositional Phrase with Compound Object

Example:

pro   *av*   *pp*   *art*   *adj*   *n*   *conj*   *n*

She dusted (under the new table and chairs).

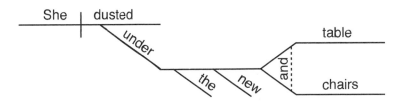

Notice that *the* and *new* are diagrammed on the line before the branch. These words modify both *table* and *chairs,* so they are not part of the branch.

H) Compound Sentence

Example:

pn   *av*   *art*   *n*   *conj*   *pn*   *av*   *pro*

Jen washed the car and Jim waxed it.

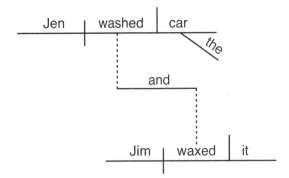

I) Multiple Compound Situations

               pn conj pn   av   conj   av   art   n

Example: Jen and Jim washed and waxed the car.

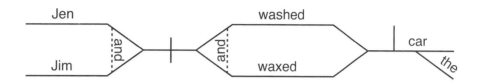

J) Diagramming Correlative Conjunctions

                 pn   pn av adj   n   adv

Example: Both Sean and Jason left their bikes outside.

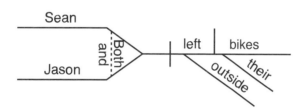

K) Compound Modifiers

               adj adj conj adj   n   av

Example: My black and white dog barked.

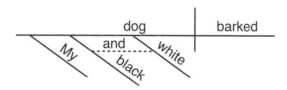

L. Three or More of Something

               pn   pn conj pn av   n

Example: John, Joe, and Jim ate lunch.

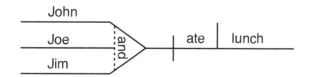

Conjunctions & Compound Situations: Exercise A

Directions

Parse and diagram the sentences below. Use the hints provided in the lesson notes to see how each compound should be diagrammed.

      adj   *n*   *conj*   *adj*   *n*   *av*   *adj*   *adj*   *n*

1) Fairy tales and nursery rhymes entertain most young children.

(See Notes A)

      adj   *n*   *av*   *av* *pro* *adj*   *adj*   *n*

2) Our parents either read or tell us these favorite stories.

(See Notes B Example 1 and J)

      adj *adj*   *n*   *av* *art*   *n* *conj* *av*   *art* *adj*   *n*   *pp*   *pro*

3) Our first teachers tell the stories and sing the nursery rhymes (with us).

(See Notes B Example 2)

      pro *av*   *adj*   *n*   *conj* *adj*   *n*

4) I loved nursery rhymes and fairy tales.

(See Notes C)

      adj   *n*   *hv*   *av* *adj*   *n*   *conj* *pro*   *n*   *pp*   *n*

5) My mother would read my brothers and me stories (before bedtime).

(See Notes D)

      pro *lv*   *adv*   *adj* *conj*   *adj*

6) We were always quiet and spellbound.

(See Notes E)

      pro   *hv*   *av*   *pro*   *pp* *art* *adj*   *n*   *pp* *adj*   *n*

7) She would read them either (in the living room) or (in our bedrooms).

(See Notes F and J)

      pro   *av*   *adj*   *n*   *pp* *art*   *n*   *conj*   *n*   *pp* *art*   *n*

8) She had special voices (for the animals and characters) (in the stories).

    (See Notes G)

      pro   *av* ————*pn*————   *conj* *adj*   *n*   *av*   *pn*

9) I loved "Little Red Riding Hood" and my brothers loved "Pinocchio."

    (See Notes H)

      pn   *pn* *conj* *pro* *lv*   *adv*   *adj*   *n*   *pp*   *adj*   *n*

10) Billy, George, and I were always perfect children (during story time)!

    (See Notes L)

Conjunctions & Compound Situations: Exercise B

Directions

Parse and diagram each sentence. Use The Process Chart and your lesson notes if you need help.

—————pn————— conj adj n av art n pp n pp adj n
1) Little Red Riding Hood and her mother packed a basket (with cookies) (for her grandma).

art n pp adj n av pp art n conj pp art n
2) The path (to Grandma's house) went (through the forest) and (up the hill).

—————pn————— av conj av pp art adj n
3) Little Red Riding Hood ran and skipped (down the forest path).

art ——pn—— av pp art n conj —————pn————— av adv
4) The Big Bad Wolf waited (behind a tree), and Little Red Riding Hood skipped past.

art ——pn—— av pp art n conj pp n pp —————pn—————
5) The Big Bad Wolf jumped (from the bushes) and (in front) (of Little Red Riding Hood).

art n av —————pn————— art n conj n pp adj n
6) The wolf asked Little Red Riding Hood the purpose and destination (of her journey).

pro hv av pp adj n conj pro lv adv adj pp pro
7) "I am going (to my grandma's), and I am not afraid (of you)!"

—————pn————— av adj n conj av adj n
8) Little Red Riding Hood grabbed her basket and continued her journey.

adj n av adj adj pp pro
9) Her grandma looked both big and strange (to her).
⤢ conj ⤢

art ——pn—— av pp —————pn————— conj av pro adv
10) The Big Bad Wolf jumped (at Little Red Riding Hood) and frightened her badly.

Fill in the blank

11) Two or more subjects in a sentence is called a _____ .

compound subject

12) When the noun before the verb means the same thing as the noun after the verb, the kind of verb you have is _____ .

a linking verb

13) An adverb can modify _____ , _____ , or _____ .

a verb, an adjective, another verb

Conjunctions & Compound Situations: Exercise C

Directions

Parse and diagram each sentence. Use The Process Chart and your lesson notes if you need help.

                adj   *n*   *adj*   *n*   *av*   *n*   *n* *conj*   *n*

1) <u>Not only</u> fairy tales <u>but also</u> nursery rhymes teach <u>children</u> values and lessons.

        adj   *adj*   *adj*   *n*   *hv*   *av*   *pp* ——————*pn*————— *conj* *art*

2) Many beloved European <u>tales</u> were written (by Hans Christian Andersen and the

        ————*pn*————

Brothers Grimm).

     ————————*pn*————————   *av* ————*pn*————   *conj*   ————*pn*————

3) Hans Christian Andersen <u>wrote</u> "The Ugly Duckling" and "The Little Mermaid."

     art ————*pn*————   *av* *pro* ————*pn*————   *conj*   ————*pn*————

4) The Brothers Grimm gave us "Little Red Riding Hood" and "<u>Hansel and Gretel</u>."

     ————————*pn*————————   *hv* *av* *pp*   *pn*   *conj* *art* ————*pn*————   *hv*   *av*

5) Hans Christian Andersen was born (in <u>Denmark</u>), and the Brothers Grimm were born

    pp   *pn*

(in Germany).

      adj   *adj* *n* *conj*   *adj*   *n*   *lv*   *n*   *pp* *art* *adj*   *adj*   *n*

6) These fairy tales and nursery rhymes are <u>examples</u> (of the strong European influence)

    pp *adj*   *adj*   *n*

(in our country's culture).

     pro *pp* *adj* *adj*   *n*   *av*   *pp*   *pn* *conj*   *adj*   *n* *hv* *av* *pp* *adj*   *n*

7) <u>Many</u> (of our fairy tales) come (from Europe), but children's stories are told (in all countries)

    conj *pp* *adj*   *n*

and (in all cultures).

```
        adj      adj      n     av    pp     pn      pn     pn    conj  art  ——pn——
```
8) Other <u>popular</u> stories come (from China, India, Africa, and the Middle East).

```
            adv      pro pp  pro   av   art  adj     n     conj    n    pp     n
```
9) <u>Interestingly,</u> all (of them) teach the same values and lessons (to children).

```
        adj     adj     n     lv     adj    pp    n     adj conj  adj
```
10) These human values are <u>common</u> (to cultures) far and wide.

Fill in the blank

11) A noun is a word that _____ .

describes a person, place, thing, or idea

12) The articles in English are _____ .

a, an, and the

13) An antecedent is _____ .

the word the pronoun takes the place of

14) In a *noun-linking verb-adjective* pattern, the adjective is called the _____ .

predicate adjective

15) List three jobs that a noun can do:

_____ ,

_____ ,

or_____ .

subject, predicate nominative, direct object, indirect object, object of the preposition
(any three of these)

Directions

Write what jobs the underlined words are doing in each sentence. Choose your answer from among the following:

subject	object of the preposition	verb
modifier	direct object	indirect object
predicate nominative	predicate adjective	

Sentence #	Word	Job
1	children	*indirect object*
2	tales	*subject*
3	wrote	*verb*
4	"Hansel and Gretel"	*direct object*
5	Denmark	*object of the preposition*
6	examples	*predicate nominative*
7	Many	*subject*
8	popular	*modifier*
9	Interestingly	*modifier*
10	common	*predicate adjective*

Application & Enrichment

Starting a Sentence with a Conjunction

Sometimes grammar rules that had been taught in the past are now outdated. Others are just plain wrong! So let's just ignore them all, right? Well, no, it's not that easy. There are many people who have learned the old incorrect or outdated rules. The problem is that these people may be potential employers, your college professors, or other people who have authority to make judgments about you in some way. If your grammar is wrong in their eyes, then it might as well be wrong. They will probably judge your writing by the rules they believe to be correct.

That's why, sometimes, you will need to stick to these outdated rules when a situation calls for "formal writing." This is the kind of writing that is expected when communicating with and within most schools, industries, and businesses. For example, academics and scientists almost always use formal writing for their research papers, articles, and dissertations. College professors often look for formal language in papers for their classes. The grammar of formal writing changes much more slowly than informal writing or language, and these old rules still apply. Think of following these outdated rules as one way that you need to change your writing for a particular audience or situation.

One of the grammar "rules" that many people believe but that is actually incorrect is this:

> *Do not start a sentence with a conjunction!*

Some people have been taught that it creates a sentence fragment. But it doesn't; not automatically, anyway. As long as the conjunction is followed by a complete sentence, it's grammatically correct to begin a sentence with one!

Subordinate and correlative conjunctions frequently start sentences.

Example: *Because* there was nothing good on TV, *I read my book for a while*.

Because is the subordinate conjunction, but it doesn't come immediately before the complete sentence *I read my book for a while*. The complete sentence doesn't need to immediately follow the conjunction.

Example: *Either* he goes *or* I go!

In this case, there's a complete sentence following each part of the conjunction.

That leaves coordinating conjunctions, such as *and*, *but*, and *or* (and the others listed in the notes for this lesson). The rule against starting a sentence with one of them may be outdated. But there are two rules to follow if you want to try it.

1)   The sentence needs to relate to the information before it. Conjunctions join things that are equal or relate them in some way. Even at the beginning of a sentence, they still do the same job.

2)   There must be an independent clause following the coordinating conjunction—no sentence fragments! It doesn't need to immediately follow the conjunction, but it needs to be somewhere in the sentence.

Example: Many people enjoy cilantro in their salsa and find it delicious. But others think it
                      tastes like soap and recoil in disgust.

1) Sentence 2 relates to Sentence 1. Both sentences are talking about cilantro in salsa. Sentence 2
        uses *But* to show that it contains information that contrasts with Sentence 1. (Think about what
        the conjunctions mean; see this lesson's notes for more information.)

2) Sentence 2 contains an independent clause (or complete sentence). It has a subject (*others*) and a
        verb (actually, two: *think* and *recoil*).

Starting a sentence with a conjunction can be used to:

- add emphasis or impact

  I won the baking contest. And I've only been baking for eight months!
  (*compare this to using a comma:* I won the baking contest, and I've only been baking for eight
  months! *It still means the same thing, but the added emphasis on the short time that I've been
  baking is lost.*)

- imitate the natural flow of conversation

  "Hi, Mary! It's been a while. So how have you been?"

Be careful not to overdo it, or it can lose its effectiveness. If you have multiple sentences in a row
beginning with conjunctions, it can seem very choppy to readers. This passage is grammatically
correct, but it leaves you almost breathless after reading it:

  So it's almost Christmas. And I was thinking about what to get for Mom. But I don't have a lot of
  money. So I tried to think of something I could give her for free. And I thought maybe I could
  clean the entire house for her. Or maybe I could do the laundry every week. But I'm still not sure
  what to give her. Nor* do I have much time left!

*When using *nor* in a sentence, the subject and verb invert to question format. Notice that the verb, *do*,
comes before the subject, *I*.

Directions

Read the following pairs of sentences. Add a conjunction to the beginning of the second sentence that shows the relationship between the sentences. Use one of the FANBOYS coordinating conjunctions—*for, and, nor, but, or, yet,* or *so*—and choose the one that emphasizes the relationship.

Example: I can't wait to see the article about our fundraiser.
But (or Yet) the newspaper delivery is late today.

These conjunctions show the contrast between the two sentences. Yet *can be used anywhere that you would use* but. *Because* yet *isn't commonly used as a conjunction in modern English, it sounds more formal to the reader or listener.*

Answers will vary. Suggested answers are shown below.

1) We were hoping that the kitchen renovation would be completed by now. _____ it is not.
    Yet (or But)

2) The game came down to a 48-yard field goal with no time left on the clock. _____ the
    kicker made it!
    And

3) If Mia wants to go to the play with us, she needs to be here by 6:30. _____ she can stay
    home if she prefers. _____ I hope she decides to come with us!
    Or, But

4) No one has asked for my opinion of the new couch. _____ will I give it!
    Nor

Directions

Each of the following begins with a conjunction. If the conjunction is followed by a complete sentence, write *sentence* in the blank. If it is followed by a sentence fragment, write *fragment*.

5) And your little dog, too! _____ *fragment*

6) But that's just how it goes sometimes. _____ *sentence*

7) Or we could always help at a soup kitchen for Thanksgiving. _____ *sentence*

8) For amber waves of grain. _____ *fragment*

9) Yet another reality television show. _____ *fragment*

Conjunctions & Compound Situations: Assessment

Directions

Parse and diagram the sentences below. Use The Process Chart and your notes if you need help.

Each correctly identified word or prepositional phrase is worth one point.

       n   hv   av   adj   n   conj   adj   n   pp adj   n

___ **1)** <u>Parents</u> should read fairy tales and nursery rhymes (to their <u>children</u>).
12

         hv   n   av   adj   n   pro av   adj   adj   n   adv

___ **2)** <u>Not only</u> do children love these <u>stories</u>, <u>but</u> they learn many valuable lessons, too.
12

     ————*pn*———— *hv   av   n   n   conj   n   pp adj   n*

___ **3)** "The Ugly Duckling" can teach <u>children</u> kindness and tolerance (of others' differences).
11

     pn   lv   adv   adj conj   adj conj pro hv   av   pp art   n

___ **4)** Cinderella was always <u>good</u> and patient, and she was rewarded (in the end).
14

     adj adj   n   av adj   n   pp   n   conj   n conj art adj   n av adj

___ **5)** Two little pigs <u>built</u> their houses (of straw and wood), but the third pig built his
21

     n   pp   n

house (of brick).

     adj   n   conj adj   n   av adj   adj   adj adj   n

___ **6)** Good planning and hard work saved all three little <u>pigs'</u> lives.
11

     ————*pn*———— *av art   n conj   av   art adj   adj   n pp art adj   n*

___ **7)** Snow White helped the dwarfs and escaped the evil queen's plot (at the same <u>time</u>).
15

     adj   n conj   n   av pro adv   pp adj   n   conj   av   adj   n

___ **8)** Pinocchio's lies and stories led him <u>away</u> (from his father) and lengthened his nose!
15

            —————————*pn*————————   *lv art   n   pp   art   n   pp   n   conj adj   n*

__ **9)** "The Emperor's New Clothes" is a story (about the dangers) (of dishonesty and false pride).
14

           pro av   adj   adj   adj   n   pp adj   adj   n   conj   n

__ **10)** We learn many valuable life lessons (in our childhood stories and rhymes).
13

——
138

Directions

Write what job the underlined words is doing in each sentence. Choose your answer from among the following:

subject   **object of the preposition**   **verb**

modifier   **direct object**   **indirect object**

predicate nominative   **predicate adjective**

Five points each

Sentence #	Word	Job
1	Parents	*subject*
1	children	*object of the preposition*
2	stories	*direct object*
3	children	*indirect object*
4	good	*predicate adjective*
5	built	*verb*
6	pigs'	*modifier*
7	time	*object of the preposition*
8	away	*modifier*
10	We	*subject*

——
50

Fill in the blank

_____ **11)** A noun is a word that _____.

1　　　　*names a person, place, thing, or idea*

_____ **12)** The articles in English are _____.

3　　　　*a, an,* and *the*

_____ **13)** An adjective is a word that _____.

1　　　　*modifies a noun or a pronoun*

_____ **14)** A pronoun is a word that _____.

1　　　　*takes the place of a noun*

_____ **15)** An antecedent is _____.

1　　　　*the noun the pronoun stands for*

_____ **16)** A verb isn't a "real" verb unless it has a _____.

1　　　　*subject*

_____ **17)** True or false: A direct object occurs with a linking verb. _____

1　　　　*false*

_____ **18)** In a N-LV-N sentence, the second noun is called the _____.

1　　　　*predicate nominative*

_____ **19)** An adverb is a word that _____.

1　　　　*modifies a verb, adjective, or adverb*

_____ **20)** The job that prepositional phrases do is _____.

1　　　　*modifier*

_____ **21)** A word can't be a preposition unless it's in a _____.

1　　　　*prepositional phrase*

_____ **22)** Two or more subjects in a sentence is called a _____.

1　　　　*compound subject*

_____ **23)** The helping verb(s) and the main verb make up the _____.

1　　　　*verb phrase*

_____ **24)** Write an example of a correlative conjunction: _____.

1　　　　*(one of the following) either...or, neither...nor, not only...but (also), both...and*

_____ **25)** The adjective following a linking verb is called the: _____.

1　　　　*predicate adjective*

___
___

17

Diagrams

Enter score from diagramming solutions here.

$$\overline{\overline{124}}$$

$$\overline{\overline{\overline{329}}} \text{ Total Points} \quad \frac{263}{329} = 80\%$$

Reinforcing Skills

Congratulations on completing Level 3! At this point, it's important to reinforce the parsing and diagramming skills your student learned in these lessons so they aren't forgotten. Your student will use these grammar skills as they learn more complex grammatical components in Level 4.

The student worktext includes 18 reinforcement exercises and answer keys that will keep your student's parsing, diagramming, and paraphrasing skills sharp. These exercises include material from a wide variety of books, poems, and stories. While your student is working on these exercises, they might find something they would love to read!

Students should complete, then correct, each exercise on their own. Assign one exercise every other week. Remind your student to use The Process Chart and the notes if they need help. If these skills are reinforced periodically, your student will be well-prepared when it's time to start Level 4.

Lesson 3: Prepositional Phrases

Exercise A

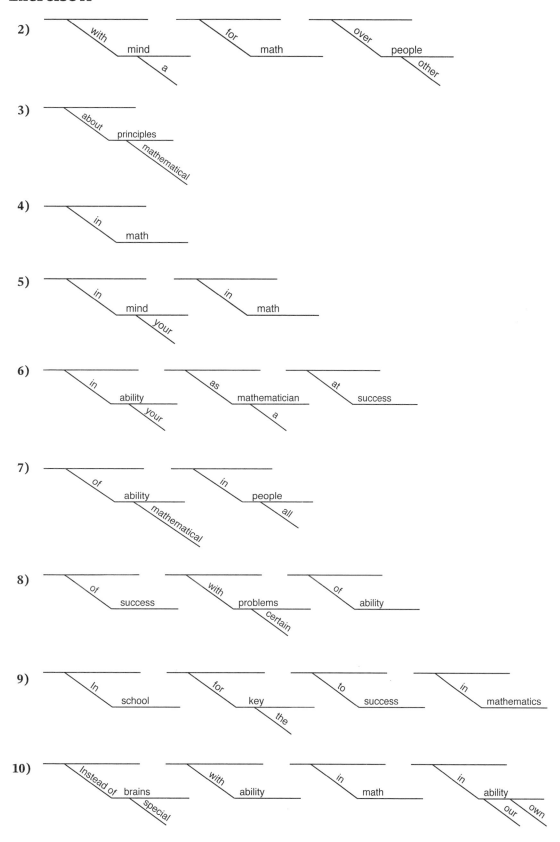

Exercise B

1)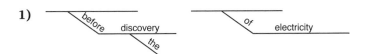

2)

3)

4)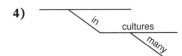

5)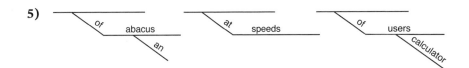

6)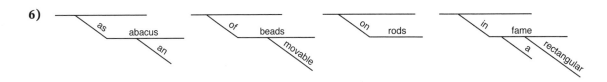

7)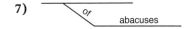

8)

9)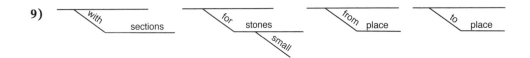

10)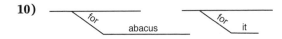

Exercise C

1)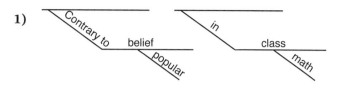

2)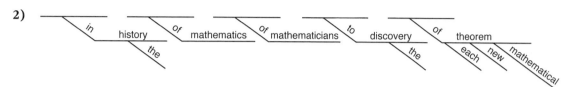

3)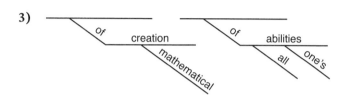

4)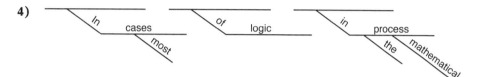

5)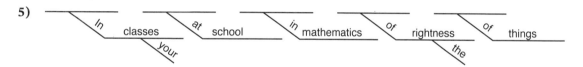

6)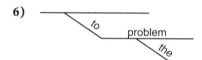

7)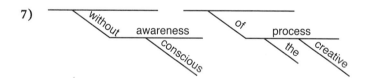

8)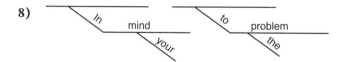

9)

10)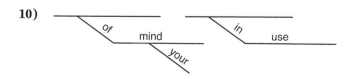

Assessment

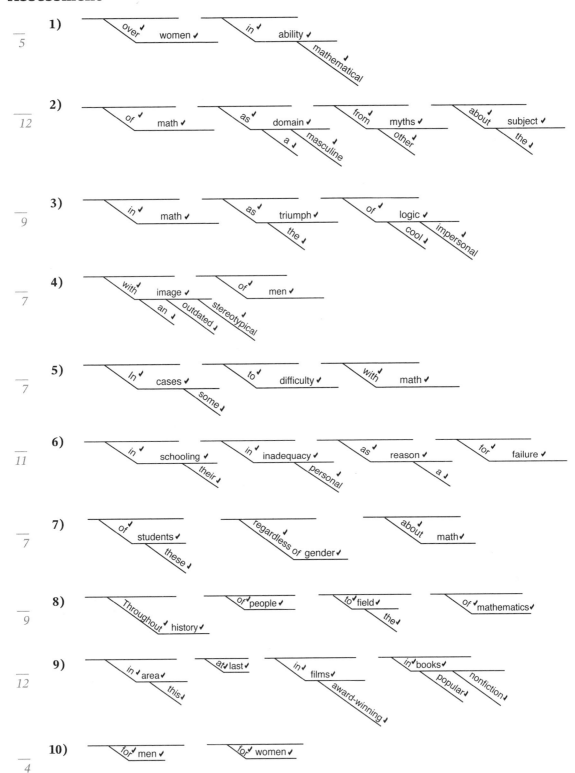

1) $\dfrac{}{5}$

2) $\dfrac{}{12}$

3) $\dfrac{}{9}$

4) $\dfrac{}{7}$

5) $\dfrac{}{7}$

6) $\dfrac{}{11}$

7) $\dfrac{}{7}$

8) $\dfrac{}{9}$

9) $\dfrac{}{12}$

10) $\dfrac{}{4}$

Diagrams

Transfer diagraming points to lesson assessment.

═══ *Total Points*

83

Lesson 4: Subject & Verb

Exercise A

1)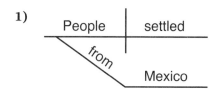

2)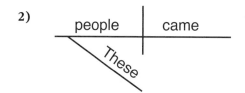

3)

4)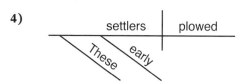

5)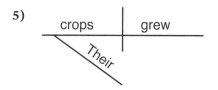

6)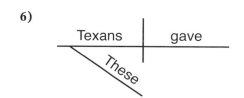

7)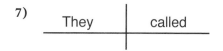

8)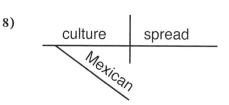

9)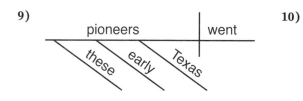

10)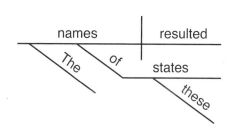

Exercise B

1)

2)

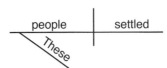

3)

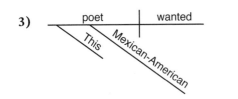

4)

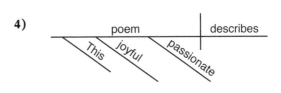

5)

6)

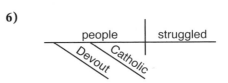

7)

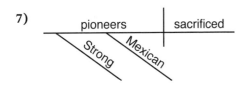

8)

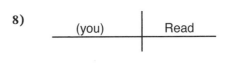

9)

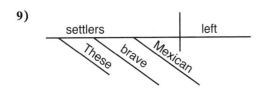

10)

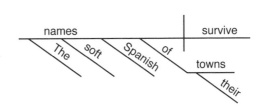

Exercise C

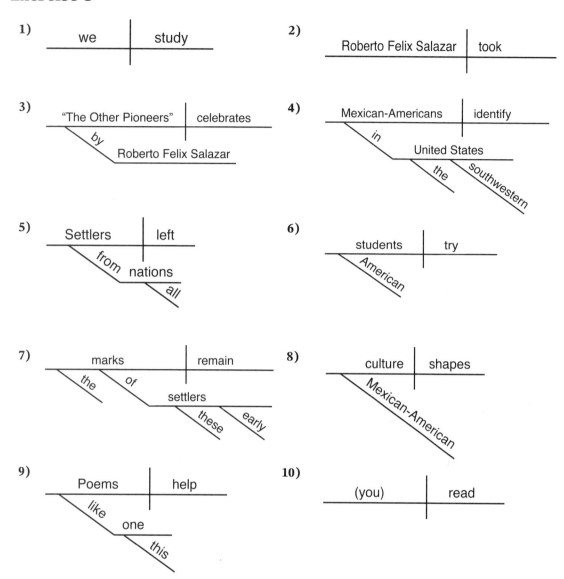

1) we | study

2) Roberto Felix Salazar | took

3) "The Other Pioneers" | celebrates
   by Roberto Felix Salazar

4) Mexican-Americans | identify
   in United States the southwestern

5) Settlers | left
   from nations all

6) students | try
   American

7) marks | remain
   the of settlers these early

8) culture | shapes
   Mexican-American

9) Poems | help
   like one this

10) (you) | read

Assessment

Each check mark represents one point. Remember that the first word of the sentence should be capitalized in the diagram.

Beginning in this lesson, a prepositional phrase—properly diagrammed and attached to the correct word—is worth one point.

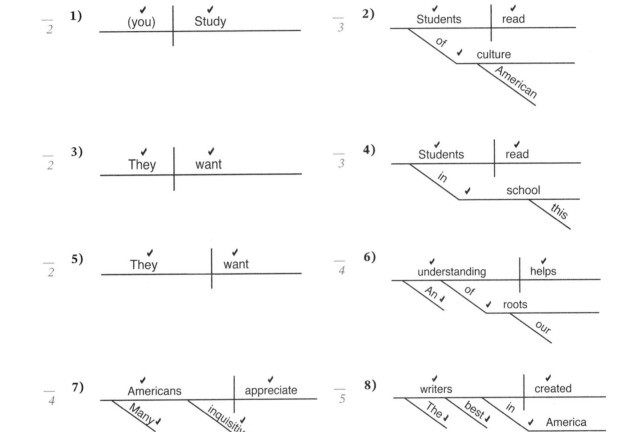

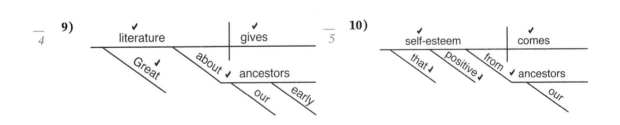

Diagrams

Transfer diagraming points to lesson assessment.

═══ *Total Points*
34

Lesson 5: Adverbs

Exercise B

1)

2)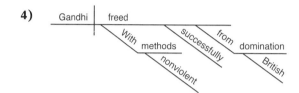

3)

4)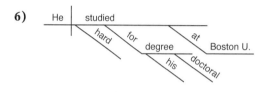

5)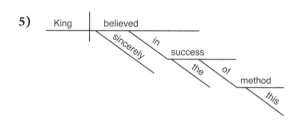

6)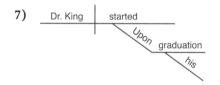

7)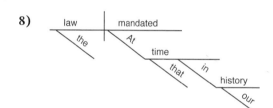

8)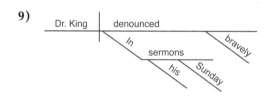

9)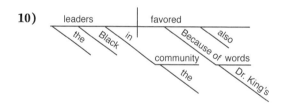

10)

Exercise C

1)
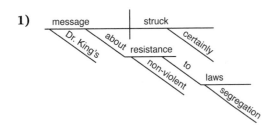

2)
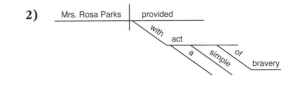

3)
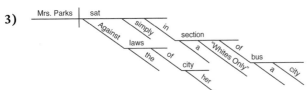

4)
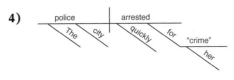

5)
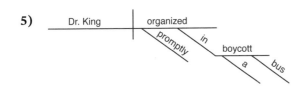

6)
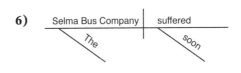

7)
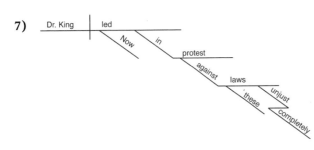

8)
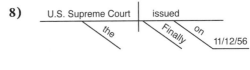

9)

10)
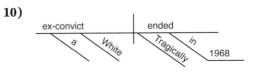

Assessment

5 **1)**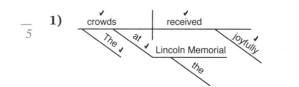

3 **2)**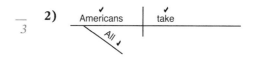

6 **3)**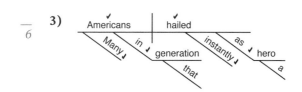

4 **4)**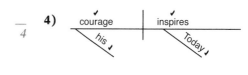

2 **5)** Dr. King | emphasized

6 **6)**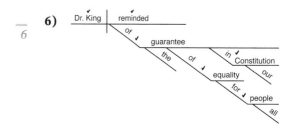

6 **7)**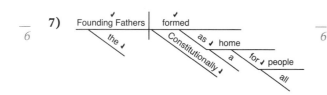

6 **8)**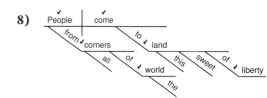

6 **9)**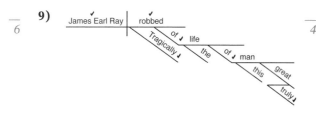

4 **10)**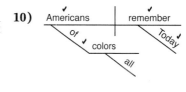

Diagrams

Transfer diagraming points to lesson assessment.

═══ *Total Points*
48

Lesson 6: Sentence Patterns 1 & 2

Exercise A

1)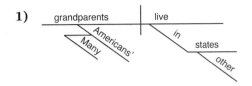

2)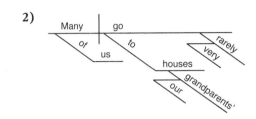

3)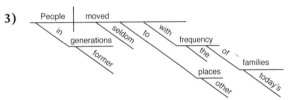

4)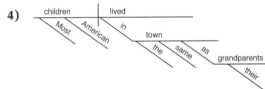

5)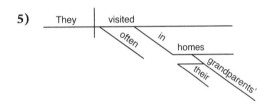

6)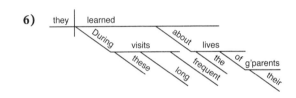

7)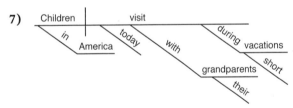

8)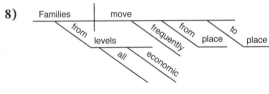

9)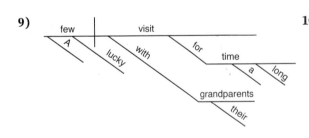

10)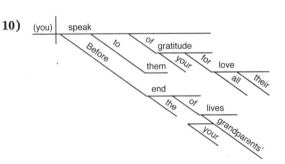

Exercise B

1)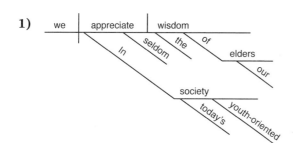

2)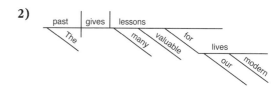

3)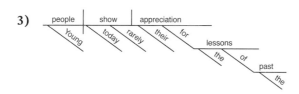

4)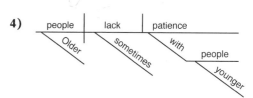

5)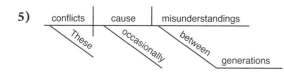

6)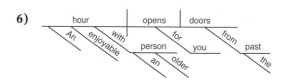

7)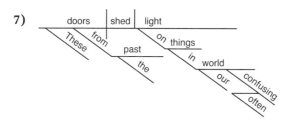

8)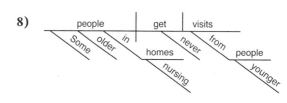

9)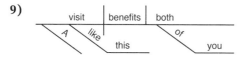

10)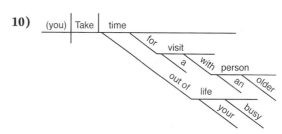

Exercise C

1)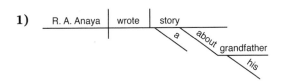

2)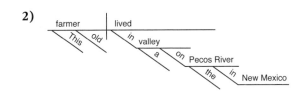

3)

4)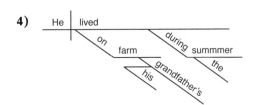

5)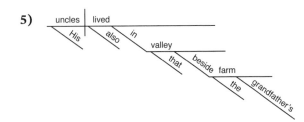

6)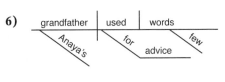

7)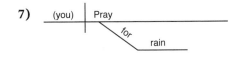

8)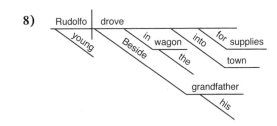

9)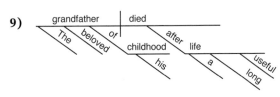

10)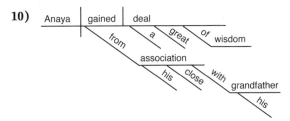

Assessment

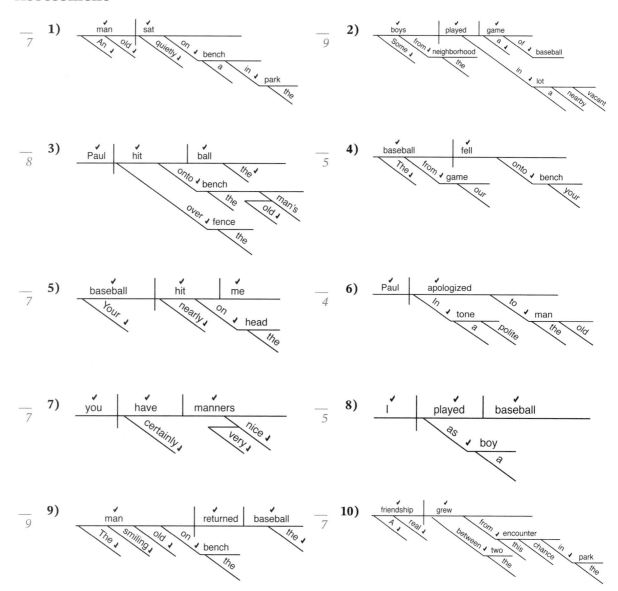

—
7   **1)**

—
9   **2)**

—
8   **3)**

—
5   **4)**

—
7   **5)**

—
4   **6)**

—
7   **7)**

—
5   **8)**

—
9   **9)**

—
7   **10)**

Diagrams

Transfer diagraming points to lesson assessment.

═══ *Total Points*
68

Lesson 7: Sentence Pattern 3

Exercise B

1)
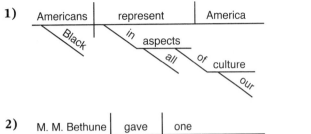

2)
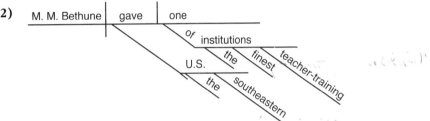

3)
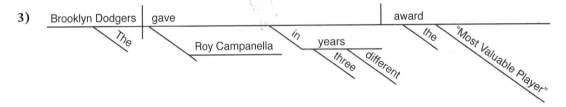

4)
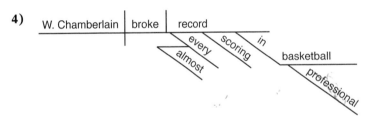

5)
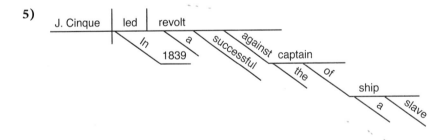

Exercise B

6)
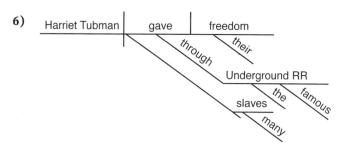

7)
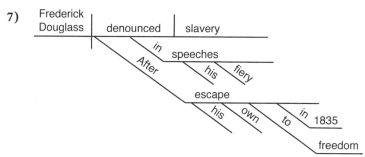

8)
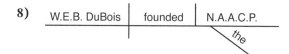

9)
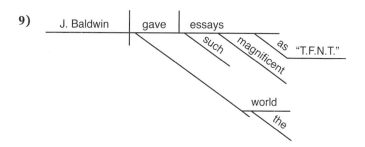

10)
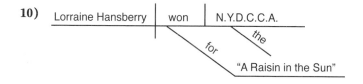

Exercise C

1)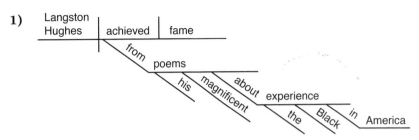

2)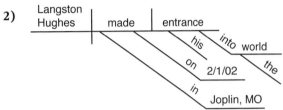

3)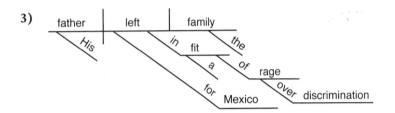

4)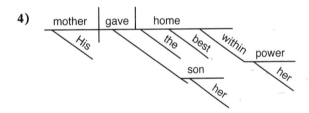

5)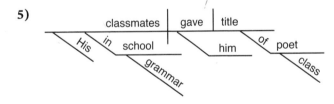

Exercise C

6)

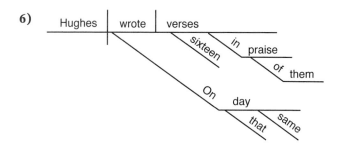

7)

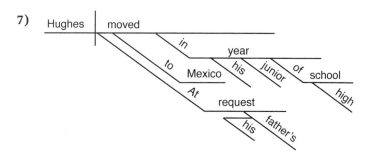

8)

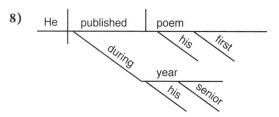

9)

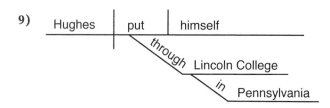

10)

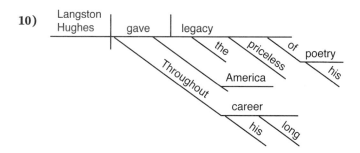

Assessment

A note on scoring:

Your student may occasionally disagree with our placement of modifiers, especially prepositional phrases. For example, in sentence #1, does "in all areas of American culture" tell you which gifts? Or does it tell how Black Americans gave them? You could move "in all areas of American culture" to the beginning of the sentence and it would make sense. The same is true of the prepositional phrase "in America" in sentence #6. If your student can make a logical argument for their placement of a modifier using the grammar rules they have learned to this point, give them credit even if it is different from the solution provided.

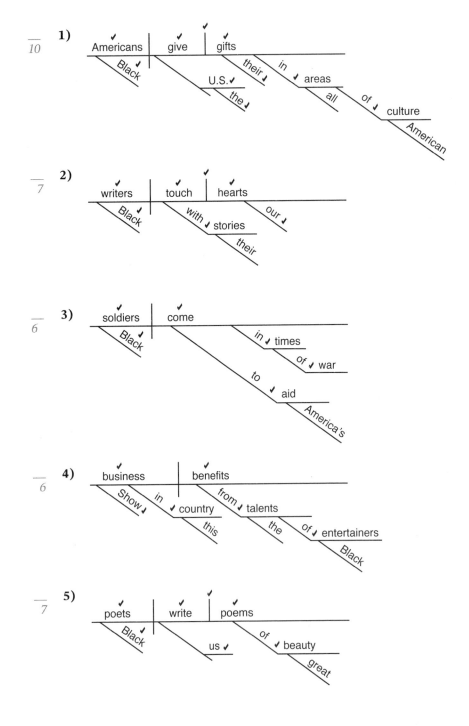

— 10   **1)**

— 7   **2)**

— 6   **3)**

— 6   **4)**

— 7   **5)**

Assessment

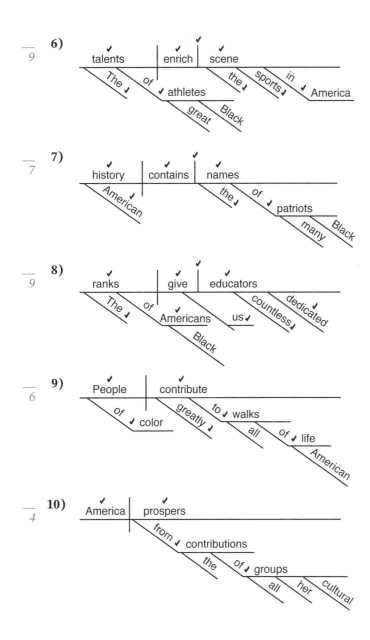

6) $\frac{}{9}$

7) $\frac{}{7}$

8) $\frac{}{9}$

9) $\frac{}{6}$

10) $\frac{}{4}$

Diagrams

Transfer diagraming points to lesson assessment.

═══ *Total Points*
71

Lesson 8: Linking Verbs and Sentence Patterns 4 & 5

Exercise A

1)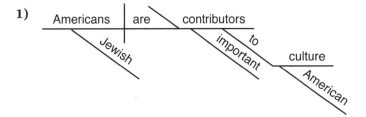

2)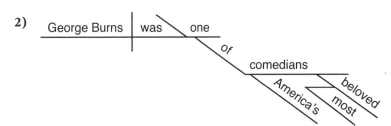

3)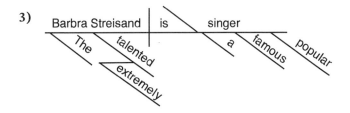

4)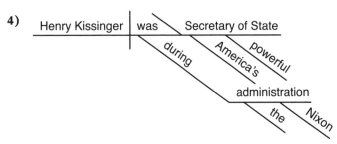

5)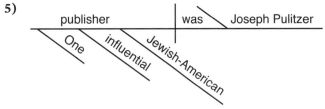

Exercise A

6)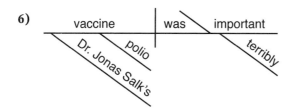

7)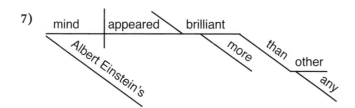

8)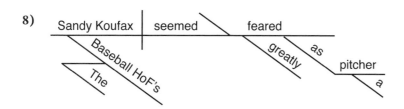

9)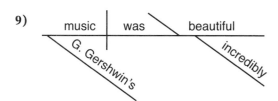

10)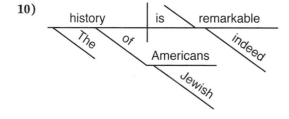

Exercise B

1)

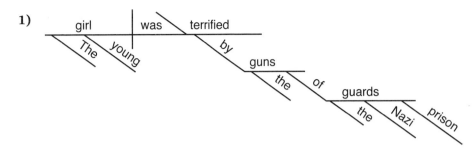

2)

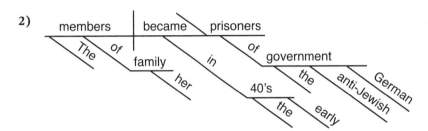

3)

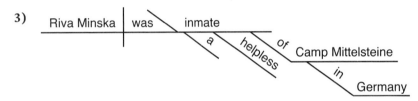

4)

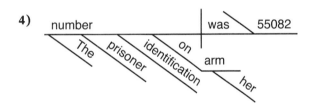

5)

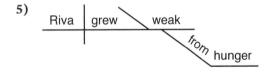

Exercise B

6)

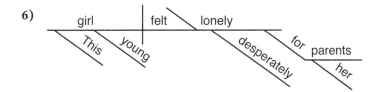

7)

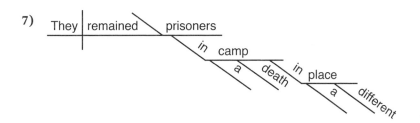

8)

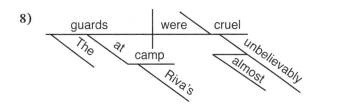

9)

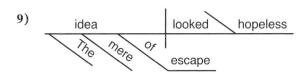

10)

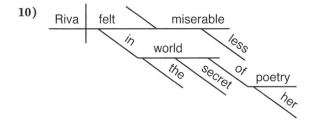

Exercise C

1)

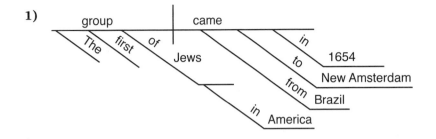

2)

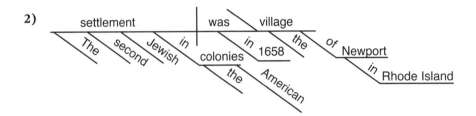

3)

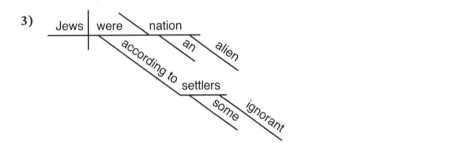

4)

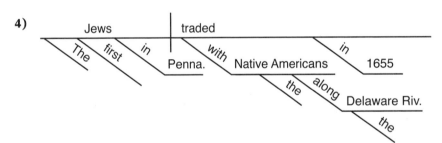

5)

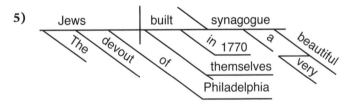

Exercise C

6)

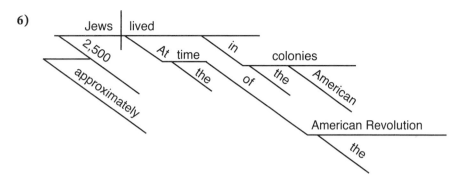

7)

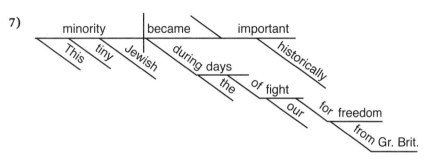

8)

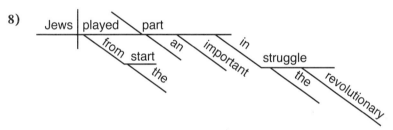

9)

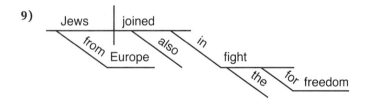

10)

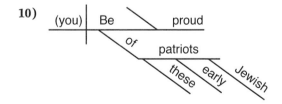

Assessment

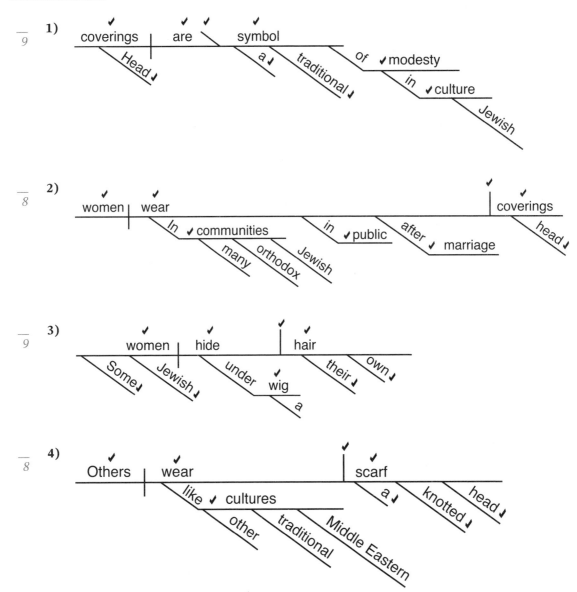

Assessment

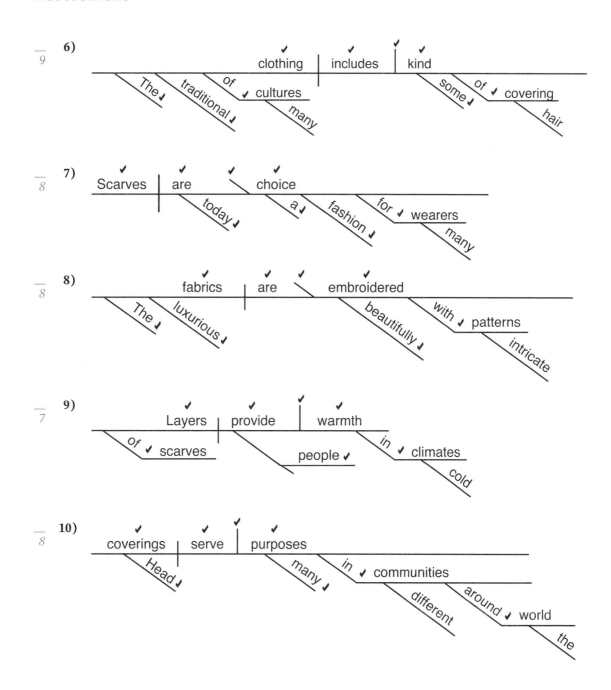

6)

7)

8)

9)

10)

Diagrams

Transfer diagraming points to lesson assessment.

══ *Total Points*
81

Lesson 9: Helping Verbs

Exercise A

Remember: Having the correct vertical or diagonal line between the verb and its complement (direct object, predicate nominative, or predicate adjective) is worth a point.

1)
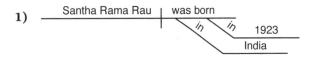

2)
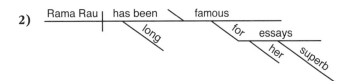

3)
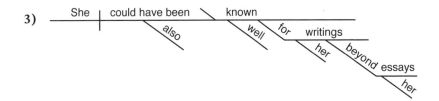

4)

5)
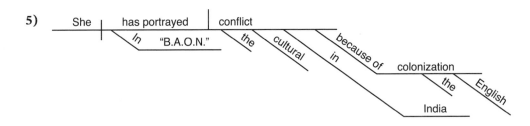

6)
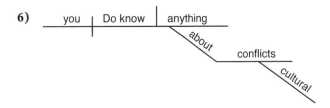

7)
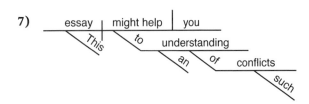

8)

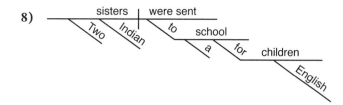

9)

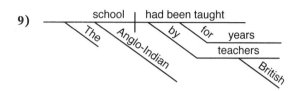

10)

Exercise B

1)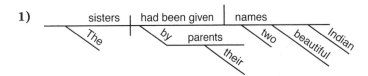

2)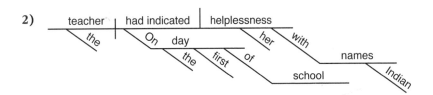

3)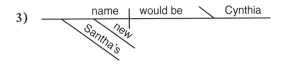

4)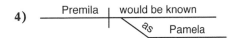

5)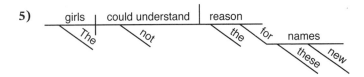

6)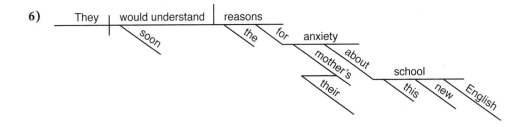

7)

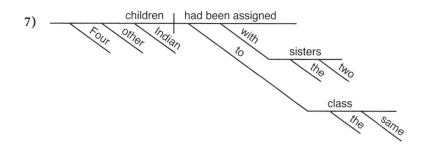

8)

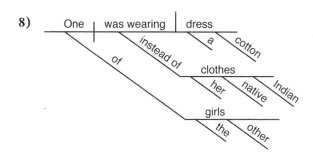

9)

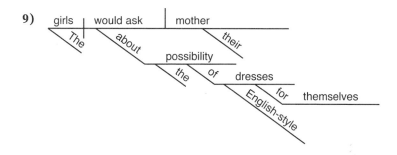

10)

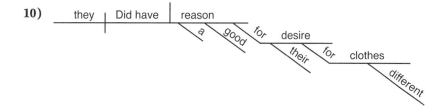

Exercise C

1)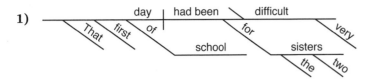

2)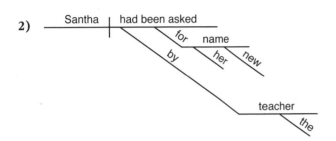

3)

4)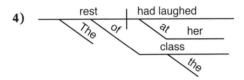

5)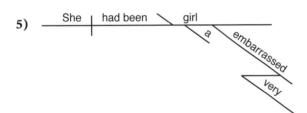

6)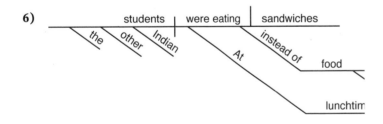

7)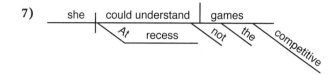

8)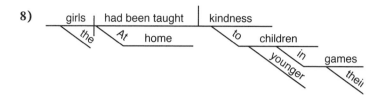

9)

10)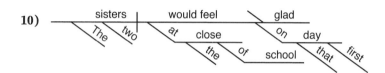

Assessment

$\frac{}{7}$ **1)**

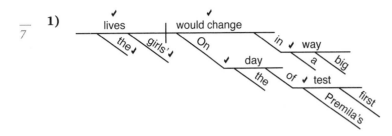

$\frac{}{5}$ **2)**

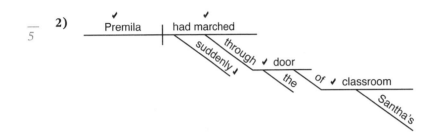

$\frac{}{6}$ **3)**

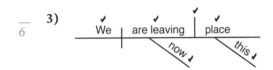

$\frac{}{6}$ **4)**

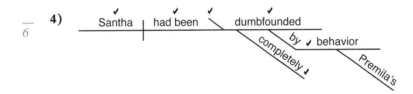

$\frac{}{7}$ **5)**

$\frac{}{7}$ **6)**

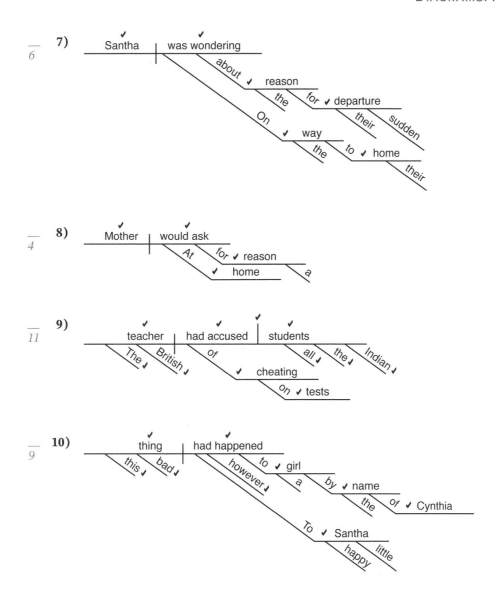

7) Santha / was wondering / about the reason for departure their sudden / On the way to home their

8) Mother / would ask / At home for reason a

9) teacher / had accused / students The British of cheating on tests all the Indian

10) thing / had happened / this bad however to girl a by name the of Cynthia To Santha happy little

Diagrams

Transfer diagraming points to lesson assessment.

68

Lesson 10: Conjunctions & Compound Situations

Exercise A

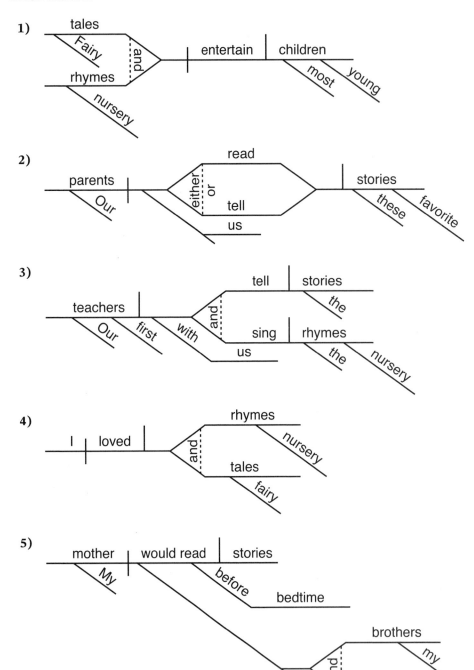

Exercise A

6)

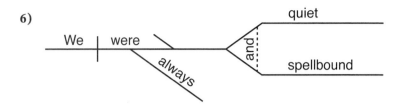

7)

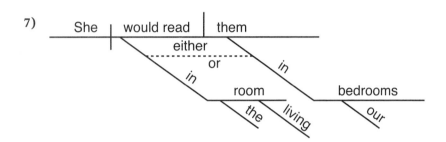

8)

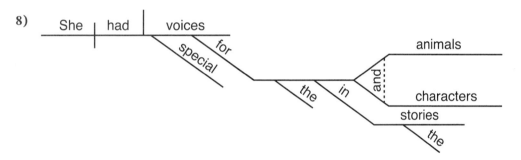

9)

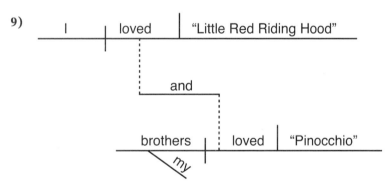

10)

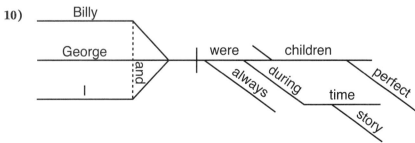

Exercise B

1)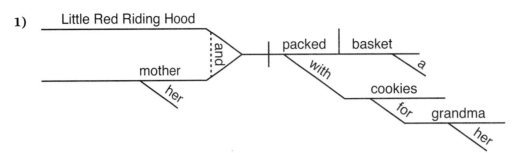

2)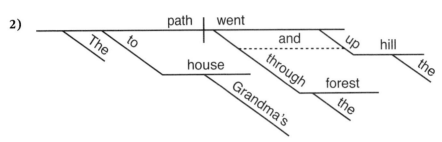

3)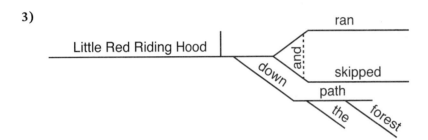

4)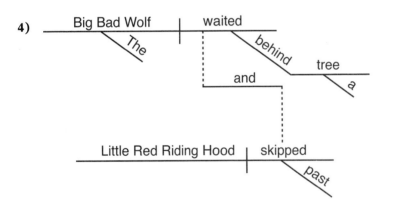

5)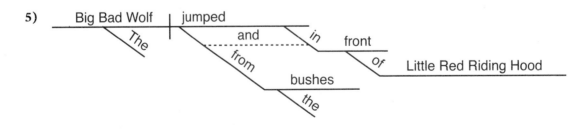

Exercise B

6)

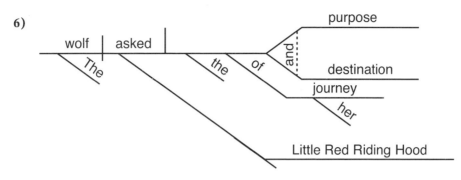

7)

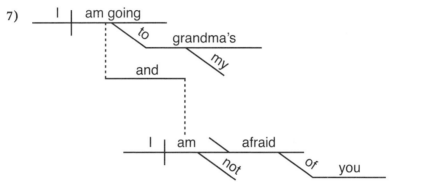

8)

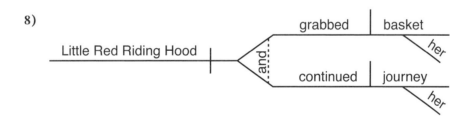

9)

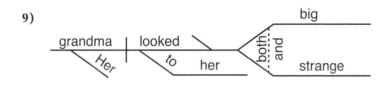

10)

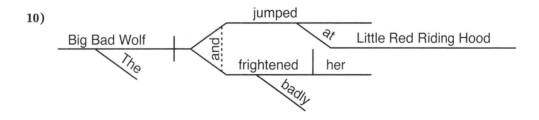

Exercise C

1)

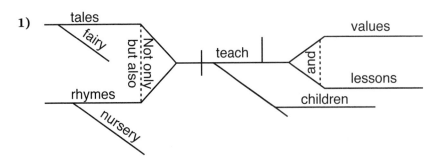

2)

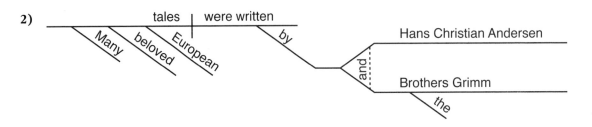

3)

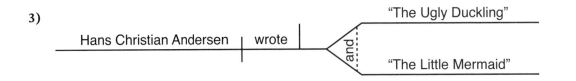

4)

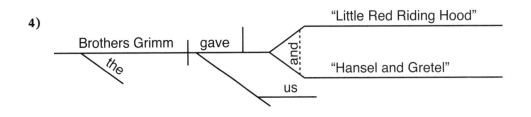

5)

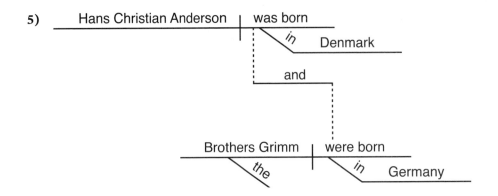

Exercise C

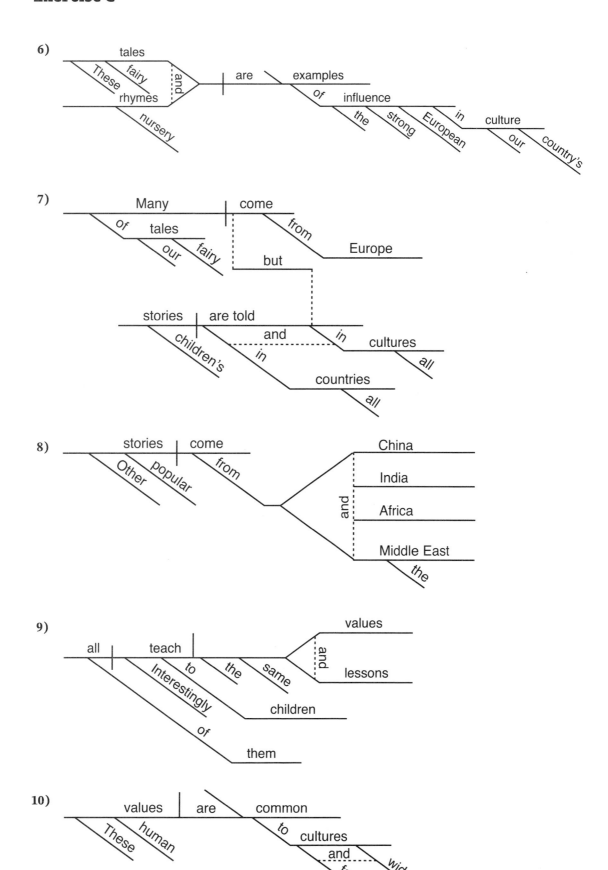

Assessment

Although prepositional phrases are usually only worth one point, for this lesson, those with compound objects will be worth more as shown.

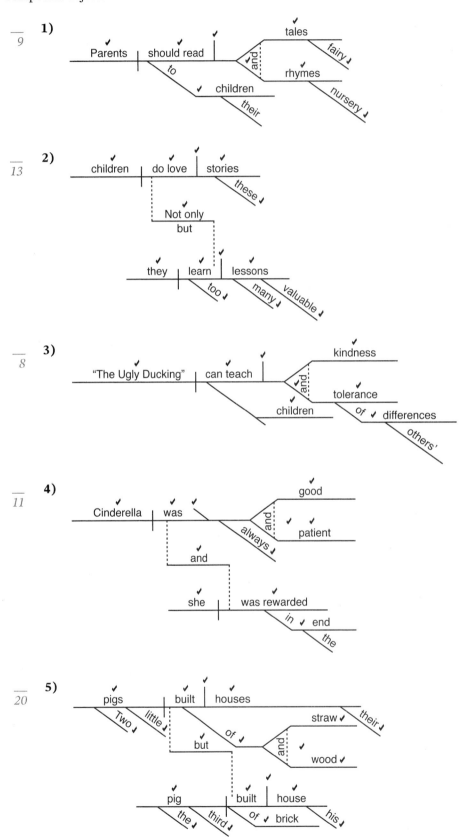

Assessment

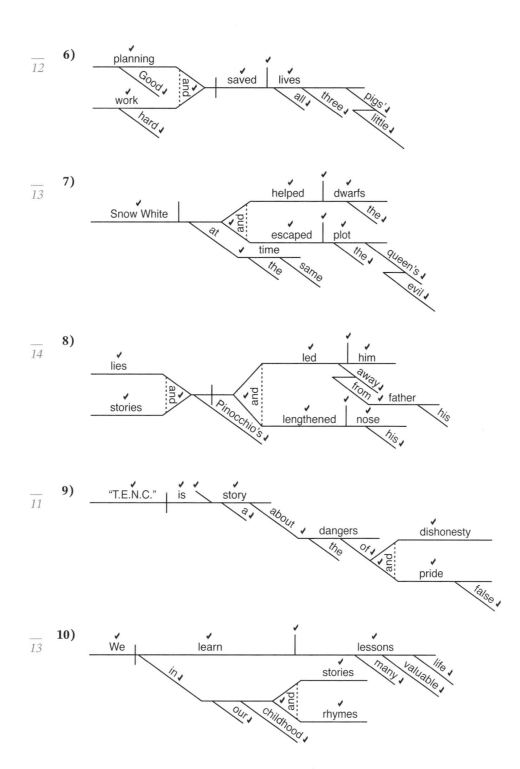

$\overline{12}$ **6)**

$\overline{13}$ **7)**

$\overline{14}$ **8)**

$\overline{11}$ **9)**

$\overline{13}$ **10)**

Diagrams

Transfer diagraming points to lesson assessment.

$\overline{\overline{}}$ *Total Points*
124

Index

Concepts are listed by lesson number.

*Indicates item is found in Application & Enrichment activity

Bibliography

Florey, Kitty Burns. Sister Bernadette's Barking Dog: The Quirky History and Lost Art of Diagramming Sentences. Orlando, FL: Harcourt, 2007.

Garner, Bryan A. Garner's Modern English Usage. Oxford: Oxford University Press, 2016.

Garner, Bryan A. The Chicago Guide to Grammar, Usage, and Punctuation. Chicago, IL: The University of Chicago Press, 2016.

Truss, Lynne. Eats, Shoots & Leaves: The Zero Tolerance Approach to Punctuation. London: Fourth Estate, 2009.